BETHLE

an

ANTHOLOGY

Compiled by
Lynn Weaver Jones

ACKNOWLEDGEMENTS

I would like to express my thanks to all those who have helped me along the way to bring this Anthology to its conclusion:

Malcolm Jones, my late husband, who provided the financial backing for the book and did the research for me but most of all encouraged me to keep going.

Cathryn Jefferson, Editor in Chief, Encourager, Enabler who transferred my handwritten manuscript into a readable Word Document.

John and Janet Angle; John and Pim Gibby; Rose Mary Whittaker, Father Michael Waters who proofread the manuscript. Plus all those who contributed to the content of the book.

Geoffrey Alcock who finally brought the book into being with the aid of the printers Sprintprint Preston Limited

ISBN 978-0-9559291-2-0
Publisher : © Lynn Weaver Jones 2019
Apt. 3 Southworth House, Preston New Road, Blackburn BB2 7AL
in co-operation with Mission to Bethlehem Publishing. Email: pimjon@aol.com

All proceeds from donation will go to Help Children in Need in Bethlehem

**Dedicated to The Palestinian Christians
who have kept, and are still keeping the light
of Christ shining in Bethlehem, His birthplace.**

Earth has many a noble city;
Bethlehem, thou dost all excel:
out of thee the Lord from Heaven
came to rule His Israel.
Fairer than the sun at morning
was the star that told His birth,
to the world its God announcing
seen in fleshly form on earth.
Eastern sages at His cradle
make oblations rich and rare;
see them give, in deep devotion,
gold and frankincense and myrrh.
Sacred gifts of mystic meaning;
incense doth their God disclose,
gold the King of kings proclaimeth,
myrrh His sepulchre foreshows.
Jesus, whom the Gentiles worshipped
at Thy glad Epiphany,
unto Thee, with God the Father
and the Spirit, glory be.

Author: Aurelius Clemens Prudentius
Translator: Edward Caswall

FOREWORD

By the compiler of this Anthology

Lynn Weaver Jones

The season of Epiphany – which the Church celebrates on the 6th January each year to remember the visit of the Magi, or wise men, to Bethlehem to worship the infant Jesus and bring Him gifts of gold, frankincense and myrrh – has become very special to me. I particularly love the hymns for that season. However, the hymn shown overleaf actually changed the whole course of my life and so will always be extra special to me.

It is special because one morning in February 1981 God used that hymn to direct my steps towards that town which is known world-wide as 'The Little Town of Bethlehem.' It was the 21st of February to be precise. I, as normal, was walking down Stokes Croft to my office in Mercury House, Old Market, Bristol, where I worked for British Telecom. It was 8.15 in the morning, the traffic whizzed past me, everyone on their way to their daily labours. Suddenly, into my mind came the words – 'Earth has many a noble city, Bethlehem thou dost all excel' . . . Bethlehem, Bethlehem, Bethlehem . . . like an old-fashioned gramophone record with a needle stuck, that one word was with me all day long. Finally, as I sat in my bedroom before going to bed, my eyes focused on two things. The first was a poster on the wall showing a picture of bread and wine. 'Bethlehem in Hebrew means House of Bread', I thought to myself. The second item that caught my attention was a little book on my bedside table; the title of the book being 'Come Home' and the picture on the front was of a flock of sheep. Bethlehem – the Shepherd's Fields! My prayer that night was, 'Lord, do you really want me to go to Bethlehem?' The answer to that prayer can be found in my books – 'Who from our Mother's Arms' and 'With Countless Gifts of Love'. For, yes, God did want me to go to Bethlehem and from 1982 to 1995, with a one year sabbatical in 1992, I served the Lord at Hope Secondary School, Beit Jala, and at Bethlehem Bible College.

I left Bethlehem in November 1995 to prepare for my marriage to Malcolm H Jones, who was then Director of Helps International Ministries, Europe and the Middle East. We met at Bethlehem Bible College, but more about that later. We have returned to Bethlehem twice since then and planned to do so one more time but Malcolm's long illness and subsequent death prevented that. However, though my physical presence is no longer there, that little town has become part of me and, the Lord willing, I may well return once more. I know I have to put this book together for the Lord has laid it on my heart and when it is completed, who knows, my times are in His hands!

I am sure the hymn writer , Aurelius Clemens Prudentius, wrote the words, 'Earth has many a noble city, Bethlehem thou dost all excel' with the birth of Jesus in mind, the greatest event that has happened in the history of mankind, Bethlehem's seemingly only claim to fame. However, there is much in its history that has added to it's excellence and I know deep down in my heart I have to share these things and introduce you to the people who have, and still are having, an impact on this little town, as well as take you on a guided tour of the historical sites, and share some of the numerous hymns and carols written about it; plus some insights from my own experiences of living in the town for nearly

14 years and of others who have visited or lived in the town, both visitors and residents. Many people I talk to who have visited the present day Bethlehem have come away slightly disappointed, simply because they expected to find the picture they had created in their minds as they have read the Nativity account in the Bible. This I can understand, but I trust and pray that those reading this book will come to see that Bethlehem does have a place in history as a truly noble city and it is not the bricks and mortar that make the place but the people who have inhabited the town throughout the centuries.

PROLOGUE
BETHLEHEM: WHAT'S IN A NAME?
Most place names have a meaning, so what is the meaning of Bethlehem?
In Hebrew Bethlehem means – HOUSE OF BREAD
In Arabic Bethlehem means – HOUSE OF MEAT
Bethlehem Ephrath or Ephratah means – FERTILE AND FRUITFULNESS
Bethlehem Judah means – PRAISE

My friend, Joy Petrecz, gave me a more up-to-date meaning; she shared that Bethlehem 'is a picture of "church" life today which was given so many years ago – that we should be men and women of God, in the house of bread, feeding on the word of God so that we may be fruitful for every good work amongst those who continually praise God.'

Earth has many a noble city
Bethlehem thou dost all excel

BETHLEHEM'S BIBLICAL HISTORY
THE OLD TESTAMENT: THE MISTS OF TIME

GENESIS

The earliest mention of Bethlehem in the Bible is found in Genesis Chapter 35. God said to Jacob, 'Go up to Bethel and settle there and build an altar there to God, who appeared to you when you were fleeing from your brother Esau'.

So Jacob and his household did as God commanded and came to Luz (that is Bethel) in the land of Canaan. Jacob stayed there; buried Deborah, the nurse of Rebecca, his wife, there. Met with God again, set up a pillar of stone there and named the place where God had talked with him Bethel.

Then he and his household moved on travelling towards Mamre, near Kiriath Arba (that is Hebron) where Abraham and Isaac had stayed. While they were still some distance from Ephrath, Rachel began to give birth and had great difficulty in childbirth, the midwife said to her, 'Don't be afriad, for you have another son.' As she breathed her last - for she was dying - she named her son Ben-Oni. But his father named him Benjamin.
So Rachel died and was buried on the way to Ephrath (that is Bethlehem). Over her tomb Jacob set up a pillar and to this day that pillar marks Rachel's Tomb.

JUDGES

Biblical history concerning Bethlehem moves on to the Book of Judges and there in Chapter 12 we read of Ibzan of Bethlehem who judged Israel. He had thirty sons, gave away thirty daughters in marriage and brought in thirty daughters from elsewhere for his sons. He judged Israel for seven years and then Ibzan died and was buried at Bethlehem.

THE BOOK OF RUTH

In the period when the Judges ruled, we come to that beautiful story in the Book of Ruth. The story begins in Bethlehem with the family of Elimelech and his wife Naomi and their two sons Mahlon and Chilion, Ephrathites of Bethlehem Famine had swept across the land and there was no food in Bethlehem. Elimelech looked across to the mountains of Moab and decided to take his family there. They found food and work, the sons married Moabite women - Orpha and Ruth. Sadly Elimelech died as did his sons, leaving Naomi a widow. About this time Naomi heard that the Lord had come to the aid of His people by providing food for them and so she decided to go back to Bethlehem with her daughters in law. She realised however, that it would be difficult for them as Moabites to live in Bethlehem and tried to persuade them to stay. Orphah agreed but Ruth insisted she go with Naomi with the beautiful words of the Book of Ruth - Chapter 1 Verses 16 and 17 -

> 'Don't urge me to leave you
> or to turn back from you.
> Where you go I will go and
> where you stay I will stay.
> Your people will be my people
> and your God my God.
> Where you die I will die and
> there will I be buried.
> May the Lord deal with me,

be it ever so severely, if anything
but death separates you and me'

When Naomi realised that Ruth was determined to go with her, she stopped urging her.

So the two of them (Naomi and Ruth) went until they came to Bethlehem. When they arrived in Bethlehem, the whole town was stirred because of them and the women exclaimed, 'Can this be Naomi?'. Their arrival in Bethlehem, coincided with the beginning of the barley harvest.

As the story evolves it is clear that it wasn't just a coincidence that it was the start of the barley harvest, it was a God-incident. For the field that Ruth chose to glean the harvest in belonged to Boaz. In verses 4-8 of Chapter 2 of the Book of Ruth we read
'Just then Boaz arrived from Bethlehem and greeted the harvesters - 'The Lord be with you'. 'The Lord bless you' they called back.'
Boaz asked the foreman of his harvesters, 'Who's young woman is that?'
The foreman replied, 'She is the Moabitess who came back from Moab with Naomi'. she said, 'Please let me glean and gather among the sheaves behind the harvesters. She went into the field and has worked steadily from morning till now, except for a short rest in the shelter'.
So Boaz said to Ruth, 'My daughter, listen to me. Don't go and glean in another field and don't go away from here. Stay here with my servant girls...'

When Ruth told Naomi it was Boaz's field in which she gleaned,

Naomi knew at once this was from God, for Boaz was a close kinsman, a kinsman redeemer. So Naomi began to plan how she could arrange for Ruth to be redeemed by Boaz according to the custom of the day, which would mean that Boaz would agree to marry Ruth and provide her with a home where she would be provided for. Naomi's plans came to pass for in verse 18 of Chapter 3 Naomi says to Ruth, 'wait my daughter, until you find out what happens. For the man will not rest until the matter is settled today'. Boaz had to ensure that another kinsman redeemer was willing to relinquish his right to accept Ruth as his wife.

The negotiations were carried out in the public at the town gate of Bethlehem in the presence of the ten elders of the town. Finally the man said, 'Then I cannot redeem it because I might endanger my own estate. You (Boaz) redeem it yourself, I cannot do it'

Chapter 4 Verse 6

The deal was sealed by the man taking off his sandal and giving it to Boaz.

Then Boaz announced to the elders and all the people, 'Today you are witnesses that I have bought from Naomi all the property of Elimelech, Chilion and Mahlon. I have also acquired Ruth the Moabitess, Mahlon's widow, as my wife, in order to maintain the name of the dead with his property, so that his name will not disappear from among his family or from the town records. Today you are witnesses'

Then the elders and all those at the gates of Bethlehem said, 'We are witnesses. May the Lord make the woman who is coming into your home, like Rachel and Leah, which together built up the house of Israel. May you have standing in Ephrath and be famous in Bethlehem through the offspring the Lord gives you by this young woman, may your family be like that of Perez whom Tamar bore to Judah'. (Chapter 4 Verses 9-12)

So Boaz took Ruth and she became his wife. And the Lord enabled her to conceive and she gave birth to a son. Then Naomi took the child, laid him in her lap and cared for him. They named him Obed. He was the father of Jesse, the father of David who became King David, ancestor of the Lord Jesus.

THE BOOK OF SAMUEL (1 & 2)

The history of Bethlehem moves on and in I Samuel, Chapter 16 Verses 1-13. The Lord said to Samuel, 'How long will you mourn for Saul, since I have rejected him as King of Israel? Fill your horn with oil and be on your way, I am sending you to Jesse of Bethlehem. I have chosen one of his sons to be king'. But Samuel said, 'How can I go? Saul will hear about it and kill me'. The Lord said, 'Take a heifer with you and say, 'I have come to sacrifice to the Lord.; Invite Jesse to the sacrifice and I will show you what to do. You are to anoint for me the one I indicate'

Samuel did what the Lord said. When he arrived at Bethlehem, the elders of the town trembled when they met him. They asked, 'Do you come in peace?', Samuel replied. 'Yes, in peace, I have come to sacrifice to the Lord. Consecrate yourselves and come to the sacrifice with me'. Then he consecrated Jesse and his sons and invited them to the sacrifices.

When they arrived, Samuel saw Eliab and thought, 'Surely the Lord's anointed stands here before the Lord'.

But the Lord said to Samuel, 'Don't consider his appearance or his height,' for I have rejected him. The Lord does not look at the things man looks at. Man looks at outward appearances, but the Lord looks at the heart'. (The story goes on to share the same response to Jesse's other sons:

Abinadab to Shammah:- Jesse has seven of his sons pass before Samuel, but Samuel said to him 'The Lord has not chosen these'. So he asked Jesse, 'Are these all the sons you have?'

'There is still the youngest', Jesse answered, 'but he is tending the sheep'. Samuel said 'Send for him; we will not sit down until he arrives'.

So Jesse sent and had him brought in. David was ruddy, with a fine appearance and handsome features. Then the Lord said, 'Rise and anoint him: he is the one'.

So Samuel took the horn of oil and anointed him in the presence of his bothers and from that day on the Spirit of the Lord came upon David in power, Samuel then went to Ramah.

In I Samuel Chapter 12 Verses 12-15 we read: Now David was the son of an Ephrathite named Jesse, who was from Bethlehem in Judah. Jesse had eight sons, and in Saul's time he was old and well advanced in years.

The three eldest sons of Jesse had gone to follow Saul in battle, but David occasionally went and returned from Saul to feed his father's sheep in Bethlehem.

The book of I Samuel, Chapter 17, goes on to tell us the account of David slaying the giant Goliath. David stands before Saul and says, 'Let no one lose heart on account of the Philistine, your servant will go and fight him', Saul replied, 'You are not able to go out against this Philistine and fight him, your only a boy and he has been a fighting man from his youth'. But David said, your servant has been keeping his father's sheep. When a lion or a bear came and carried off a sheep from the flock, I went after it, struck it and rescued the sheep from its mouth. When it turned on me,

I seized it by it's hair, struck it and killed it.'
David convinced Saul that he could also kill Goliath and finally did so using five smooth stones from the brook and his sling. Because of this accomplishment Saul enquired of David, 'Whose son are you young man?' and David said, 'I am the son of your servant Jesse of Bethlehem'.

2 SAMUEL 23 Verses 13-17 tells us that David was hiding in the cave of Adullam, with his men who had deserted Saul. A troop of Philistines encamped in the Valley of Raphaim, a route to Jerusalem and their garrison was in Bethlehem. David said, 'Oh that someone would get me a drink of the water from the well near the gate of Bethlehem'. So three of David's mighty men broke through the camp of the Philistines, drew water from the well and brought it to David, but he refused to drink it, instead he poured it out before the Lord. 'Far be it from me, O Lord, to do this!' he said. 'Is it not the blood of men who went at the risk of their lives? And David would not drink it. (David regarded it as too precious to drink and offered it as a sacrifice. Ordinarily, wine was used for a drink offering).

After King David, Bethlehem is mentioned three more times in the Old Testament. 2 Chronicles 11 Verses 5-12
In the time of Rehobaom, Bethlehem became a fortified city with captains in charge and stores of food, oil and wine and shields and spears. It was a stronghold.

Chronicles also tells us that:
Bethlehems is located in the hill country of Judah, established itself as a town through the descendants of Caleb - Ephrathah -

Hur - Salma.

In the Old Testament Book of 1 Chronicles - Chapter 2 in verse 50 we read - 'These were the descendents of Caleb - The sons of Hur, the first born of Ephrathah: Shobab the father of Kiriath Jearim, Salma the father of Bethlehem and Hareph the father of Beth Cader.
In verse 54 we read: The descendents of Salma: Bethlehem.

So Ephrathah was the mother of Hur.
Hur was the father of Salma.
Salma was known as the father or founder of Bethlehem.

The chronicler recorded Caleb's genealogy because of the significance of Bethlehem, the birthplace of King David.
So Ephrathah (Ephrath) is synonymous with the town of Bethlehem.
Ephrathah the mother of Hur
Hur the father of Salma
Salma the father of founder of Bethlehem.

BOOK OF EZRAH CHAPTER 2 VERSE 21
After the exile of Babylon, Ezra tells us that 123 people from Bethlehem came back to the city.

BOOK OF MICAH CHAPTER 5 VERSE 2

Finally, in Micah, we have the link making Bethlehem part of the Old Testament and the New Testament:

'But you, Bethlehem Ephrathah though you are small among the clans of Judah, out of you will come for me one who will be ruler over Israel, whose origins are from old, from ancient times'

O little town of Bethlehem,
how still we see you lie!
Above your deep and dreamless sleep
the silent stars go by.
Yet in your dark streets shining
is everlasting light;
the hopes and fears of all the years
are met in you tonight.

For Christ is born of Mary
and, gathered all above,
while mortals sleep, the angels keep
their watch of wondering love.
O morning stars, together
proclaim the holy birth,
and praises sing to God the King
and peace to men on earth.

How silently, how silently
the wondrous gift is given!
So God imparts to human hearts
the blessings of His heaven.
No ear may hear his coming
but in this world of sin,
where meek souls will receive Him, still
the dear Christ enters in.

O Holy Child of Bethlehem,
descend to us, we pray;
cast out our sin and enter in;
be born in us today.
We hear the Christmas angels,
the great glad tidings tell.
O come to us, abide with us,
our Lord Immanuel.

Philips Brooks (1835 – 93)

THE NEW TESTAMENT: BETHLEHEM FULFILS ITS DESTINY

THE GOSPEL OF LUKE
Chapter 2: THE BIRTH OF JESUS VERSES 1-20

In those days Caesar Augustus issued a decree that a census should be taken of the entire Roman world. (This was the first census that took place while Quirinius was Governor of Syria.) And everyone went to his own town to register.

So Joseph also went up from the town of Nazareth in Galilee to Judea, to Bethlehem the town of David, because he belonged to the house and line of David. He went there to register with Mary, who was pledged to be married to him and was expecting a child. While they were there the time came for the baby to be born and she gave birth to her first born, a son. She wrapped him in cloths and placed him in a manger, because there was no room for them in the inn.

AWAY IN A MANGER
Away in a manger, no crib for a bed,
the little Lord Jesus laid down his sweet head.
The stars in the bright sky looked down where he lay,
the little Lord Jesus asleep on the hay.

The cattle are lowing, the baby awakes,
but little Lord Jesus no crying he makes.
I love thee, Lord Jesus! Look down from the sky,
and stay by my side until morning is nigh.

Be near me, Lord Jesus; I ask thee to stay
close by me for ever, and love me, I pray.
Bless all the dear children in thy tender care,
and fit us for heaven, to live with thee there.

Author (attributed to) Martin Luther (1483-1546)

THE SHEPHERDS AND THE ANGELS

And there were shepherds living out in the fields nearby, keeping watch over their flocks at night. An angel of the Lord appeared to them and the glory of the Lord shone around them and they were terrified. But the angel said to them, 'Do not be afraid. I bring you good news of great joy that will be for all the people. Today in the town of David a Saviour has been born to you; He is Christ (or Messiah) the Lord. This will be a sign to you: you will find a baby wrapped in cloths and lying in a manger.'

Suddenly a great company of the heavenly host appeared with the angel, praising God and saying,

'GLORY TO GOD IN THE HIGHEST, AND ON EARTH PEACE TO MEN ON WHOM HIS FAVOUR RESTS.'

When the angels had left them and gone into heaven, the shepherds said to one another, 'Let's go to Bethlehem and see this thing that has happened which the Lord has told us about.'

So they hurried off and found Mary and Joseph and the baby, who was lying in the manger. When they had seen him, they spread the word concerning what had been told them about this child and all who heard it were amazed at what the shepherds said to them. But Mary treasured up all these things and pondered them in her heart. The shepherds returned, glorifying and praising God for all the things they had heard and seen, which were just as they had been told.

THE GOSPEL OF MATTHEW CHAPTER 2

After Jesus was born in Bethlehem in Judea, during the time of King Herod, Magi from the east came to Jerusalem and asked, 'Where is the one who has been born King of Jews? We saw his star in the east and have come to worship him.'

When King Herod heard this he was disturbed and all Jerusalem with him. When he had called together all the people's chief priests and teachers of the law, he asked them where the Christ was to be born. 'In Bethlehem in Judea'. Then Herod called the Magi secretly and found out from the exact time the star had appeared. He sent them to Bethlehem and said, 'Go and make a careful search for the child. As soon as you find him report to me, so that I too may go and worship him'. After they had heard the King, they went on their way and the star they had seen in the east went ahead of them and it stopped over the place where the child was. When they saw the star, they were overjoyed. On coming to the house they saw the child with his mother Mary, and they bowed down and worshipped him. Then they opened their treasures and presented him with gifts of gold and of incense and myrrh. And having been warned in a dream not to go back to Herod, they returned to their country another route.

ESCAPE TO EGYPT

When they had gone, an angel of the Lord appeared to Joseph in a dream, 'Get up, he said, 'take the child and his mother and escape to Egypt. Stay there until I tell you for Herod is going to search for the child and kill him'.

So he got up, took the child and his mother during the night and left for Egypt, where he stayed until the death of Herod.

And so was fulfilled what the Lord had said through the prophet:

'Out of Egypt I called my son'.

When Herod realised that he had been outwitted by the Magi he was furious and he gave orders to kill all boys in Bethlehem and it's vicinity who were two years old and under in accordance with the time he had learned from the Magi.

Then what was said through the prophet Jeremiah was fulfilled, 'A voice is heard in Ramah, weeping and great mourning, Rachel weeping for her children and refusing to be comforted, because they are no more'.

WE THREE KINGS OF ORIENT ARE
We three kings of Orient are;
bearing gifts we traverse afar;
field and fountain, moor and mountain,
following yonder star.

Born a King on Bethlehem's plain,
gold I bring, to crown him again,
King for ever, ceasing never,
over us all to reign.

Frankincense to offer have I,
incense owns a Deity nigh,
prayer and praising, gladly raising,
worship him, God most high.

Myrrh is mine, its bitter perfume
breathes a life of gathering gloom;
sorrowing, sighing, bleeding, dying,
sealed in the stone-cold tomb.

O star of wonder, star of night,
star with royal beauty bright,
westward leading, still proceeding,
guide us to thy perfect light.

Rev. John Henry Hopkins (1820-1891)

This prophecy from Jeremiah Chapter 31 verse 15 in which Rachel, who had been entombed near Bethlehem, some thirteen centuries before the Babylonian captivity, is seen weeping for her children as they are led away to Babylon in 586 BC. In the slaughter of the male infants at the time of Christ's birth Rachel once again is pictured as mourning the violent loss of her sons.

These events probably took place some months after Jesus' birth. Several reasons may be offered to support this conclusion:
1. Joseph and Mary were living in a house.
2. Jesus is referred to as a child, not an infant.
3. Herod murdered all the male children two years and under.
4. It would have been strange for Joseph and Mary to offer the sacrifice of the poor, a pair of turtle doves or pigeons, if the wise men had just given them gold, frankincense and myrrh. Thus the wise men must have arrived after the ritual sacrifice described in Luke Chapter 2.

Note: many centuries on from Herod's massacre during excavations in the area of the Holy Nativity Church in Manger Square, an area was uncovered to reveal numerous bones which could have only been the bones of small children. These were carefully removed and reburied in the caves under St Katherine's Church, adjacent to the Church of the Holy Nativity. An altar was placed over them.

In this complex of caves can be found the Chapel of St Jerome, one of the first translators of Scripture. Also, significantly, in the same complex of caves is the cave which marks the birth place of Jesus Christ. In other words, 'the stable to which Joseph and Mary were directed because there was no room in the inn.' It is now covered by the Church of the Holy Nativity and is accessed by a flight of steps.

This section concludes the biblical references to the little town of Bethlehem. The events in the Gospel truly mark a dividing line in the history of the world. From the birth of Jesus in Bethlehem, time has been recorded as BC (Before Christ) and AD (Anno Domini, the Year of the Lord).

We have no more references of Jesus returning to Bethlehem, but the town continued to be. It has not been destroyed, it remains standing to this day.

Having introduced this book and completed stage one – the Biblical History of Bethlehem – I found myself in somewhat of a limbo, the main reason being that although we talk about the Little Town of Bethlehem, since the actual events surrounding the nativity of Jesus over 2000 years have rolled by, the life of that little town has continued to thrive and grow. It was never intended for me to write a complete history of the town itself and I finally came to understand this little book is to be a celebration of the town which has remained in world focus all those 2000 or so years because of its spiritual importance and that importance is the fact that it was the birth place of the Lord Jesus Christ.

Bethlehem has had a special place in my life since I was a child, as I am sure it has in the lives of all Christians. Although there have been pilgrims visiting the town throughout the ages many, many more would like to go but are not able to. I have been blessed more than most because I was led by the Lord to live in the town and work alongside Palestinian Christians for over 12 years, meeting and making friends from around the world as they, too, visited or worked in Bethlehem, and this is my starting point for the next section of the book. I want to share some of my own and others' experiences in the town and in closing this section give you all a break and introduce, you, to some of the people living to-day.

BRISTOL TO BETHLEHEM

As I have just explained, Bethlehem has always had a special place in my heart and one of the recurring memories of my childhood and teenage years is of cold frosty Christmas Eves and going to the midnight services at the Parish Church of the Holy Trinity in our village. During the service, when the carol 'O little town of

Bethlehem' was announced, Mum would look at me and smile. It was her favourite carol and she would often recall hearing a boy cousin, Jonty Weaver, singing the boy soprano solo of the opening verse. She would say, 'His voice is like a bell.' That carol became 'Christmas' for us. Somehow I have a feeling that it was during that period of my life that the little seed 'Bethlehem' was sown in my heart, but it didn't make itself felt until the 1970's although I didn't know what was happening – just a restlessness that something was going to happen.

In the early 1970's I applied to go as a volunteer for a month with a group going to the Edinburgh Medical Mission Hospital in Nazareth but I was considered too old! Most of the group were in their teens, I was in my thirties. Then in December 1974 in the CMJ (Churches Ministry to the Jews) Magazine I saw a tour of the Holy Land advertised for May 1975 and booked a place on that. However, on the 1st January 1975 Mum was taken ill with leukaemia and within six weeks had gone to be with her Lord. Then one January evening in 1978 I was taking my Pathfinder Group's evening in the church hall when my friend Phyl Bryant walked in and said, 'Brian Treharne from Christ Church, Cotham, is taking a tour to the Holy Land in May. Would you come with me?' The door was finally opened for my heart's desire and I was definitely going through it this time.

The brochure advertising the Pilgrimage was headed 'A Holiday of a Lifetime'. Little did I know, as I prepared to join the group, that in fact it would be for me an experience that would change the whole course of my life. I wasn't aware of that as we travelled around the Holy Land. On the first day of our tour we visited

Bethlehem and experienced the 'busyness' of the souk (market), bargained for souvenirs and just one memory of that visit stands out. We entered the very small door of the Church of the Holy Nativity, went down into the cave that marks the birthplace of Jesus, and before we left we climbed some steps onto the roof and as we looked down onto the scene below us we sang the carol 'O little town of Bethlehem' which was indeed a very moving experience for me. Then it was back to Jerusalem to see more sights before checking in to our hotel for the night. On our last day in Jerusalem, very early in the morning, a small group of us left the hotel – the Pilgrim's Palace, near Damascus Gate – took taxi cabs to the top of the Mount of Olives and walked down the narrow pathway that Jesus would have come down on that first Palm Sunday, riding on a donkey. As our group neared the Garden of Gethsemane, at the foot of the Mount of Olives, around the corner came a young Arab boy with his flock of sheep and goats. He was riding a donkey and had a palm branch in his hand. Seeing a group of English tourists his reaction was quick. Here was a chance to make a few shekels by having his photograph taken with them. He jumped off the donkey, threw down the palm branch and picked up the tiniest lamb in his flock. He walked up to me, placed the lamb in my arms, put his arm around me and stood with a big grin on his face. A happy holiday memory or was it something more? It was definitely something more, for on returning home the Lord began to lead me in so many different ways, beginning with the scripture from John 21 verse 15 –

When they had finished eating, Jesus said to Simon Peter, Simon son of John, do you truly love me more than these, 'yes Lord', he said, 'you know that I love you'. Jesus said, 'feed my lambs'.

It was to take four years before I finally found out which 'lambs' Jesus wanted me to feed, including another tour of the Holy Land. I returned from that tour and settled back into my life in Bristol, helping to care for my father who was 84 years old, doing my job at British Telecom and being fully involved in my church and youth work.

Until slowly but surely it became clear to me that the 'lambs' Jesus wanted me to feed were located in the town of Bethlehem and the two adjoining towns that make up the Christian Triangle of Bethlehem – Beit Jala – Beit Sahour.
It began to be made very clear to me one cold winter morning as I was walking to work down Stokes Croft to my office in Mercury House, Old Market, Bristol. It was the 21st February 1981 to be precise.

The week before I had gone to the mid-week Bible Study at church and the vicar, Reverend Ray Brazier, had asked us to turn to John 21 in our bibles. There it was again, verse 15 – 'FEED MY LAMBS.'
In my inner being, and almost in desperation, I cried out to the Lord, 'I am willing to feed YOUR lambs, Lord, but please show me which lambs YOU want me to feed!'

So here I was one week later, going about my normal business, walking along one of the busiest roads in Bristol at 8.15 am when into my mind came an Epiphany hymn –

EARTH HAS MANY A NOBLE CITY
BETHLEHEM THOU DOST ALL EXCEL
Bethlehem – Bethlehem – Bethlehem . . . like an old-fashioned gramophone record with the needle stuck. That one word was with me all day long until finally that evening I went up to my room, sat in my chair and quieted myself. There in the stillness my eyes focused on two things. The first was a poster on the wall of bread and wine. 'Bethlehem in Hebrew means House of Bread', I thought to myself. The second item that caught my attention was a little book on my bedside table which had been sent to me for Christmas. The title of the book was 'Come Home' and the picture on the front was of a flock of sheep – Bethlehem, the Shepherds' Fields!

My response, 'Lord, do you really want me to go to Bethlehem? No, I can't be hearing you right. I don't want to go to Bethlehem,' were the thoughts tumbling around in my mind for the next two days. Finally I got out the atlas to see if there were any other Bethlehems in the world. There are, but on the evening of Saturday 21st March 1981 I knew without a doubt that it was Bethlehem-Ephratah, David's City, that the Lord wanted me to go to feed His lambs.

The house was quiet, my father and I sat by the fire reading. I picked up the book of Bible Readings used in my church to read the scriptures which would be read at the church service the next day, Sunday 22nd March. I didn't get beyond the first verse – 'THE LORD SAID TO ABRAM, LEAVE YOUR NATIVE LAND, YOUR RELATIVES AND YOUR FATHER'S HOUSE AND GO TO A COUNTRY THAT I AM GOING TO SHOW YOU.'

(Genesis 12 verse 1)

I knew without a shadow of doubt that the Lord wanted me to go to Bethlehem. As I closed the book my sister Dorothy, whose home Dad and I shared, came into the room and said, 'There is a lovely programme about Israel on the television.' My father switched on the television and we were just in time to see the end of the programme. The author, Amos Oz, was seated on the grass, surrounded by children, telling them a story.

The next morning I went to church in a dream. As I sat in the congregation and looked around I thought to myself, 'I don't want to leave my father's house, my family and my friends.'

The rest of the day passed with my mind in turmoil until it came time to go to bed. I opened my copy of Living Light to read the portion for the evening of Sunday 22nd March and this is what I read,

'You will need the strong belt of truth and the breastplate of God's approval.

You will need faith as your shield to stop fiery arrows aimed at you by Satan.

And you will need the helmet of salvation and the sword of the Spirit, which is God' word.

The Lord is with you.

I will make you strong.

Go . . . I am sending you.

'But I can't just go to Bethlehem', I heard myself saying a few evenings later as I shared with Ray and Liz Brazier (my vicar and his wife). 'I don't know anyone in Bethlehem and for my father's sake I have to know where I am going.'

'Right', said Ray, 'start knocking on doors and if you are meant to go the right door will open.'

I began knocking on doors and finally received a letter from Ken Burnett, Prayer for Israel. 'If you still feel it is Bethlehem you are being called too, we have heard of a Bible College which has just opened in Bethlehem. If you would like to write to them we will see they get your letter.'

Like Gideon, I put out a fleece. I asked the Lord that 'Bethlehem' would be mentioned each day of the coming week. Bearing in mind this was July 1981, and nothing to do with Christmas, it did.

I finally sat down and wrote to Bethlehem Bible College, letting them know that God wanted me to come to Bethlehem but I didn't know what He wanted me to do there. I told them I was a qualified Nursery Nurse and a secretary and asked if they knew anyone who could use my help.

The airmail letter I received in reply was dated 17th August 1981. It was signed by Solomon Douhne, Headmaster Hope School, Beit Jala and Alex Awad, Acting President, Bethlehem Bible College.

The gist of the letter was to say that both Hope School and Bethlehem Bible College were in need of an English speaking secretary. They could not support me financially, I would have to go as a volunteer, but they could provide free room and board. They asked for letters of recommendation from my Pastor and my place of work and concluded by saying –

'As a general requirement we expect our workers to be called by God to this ministry, to love the Lord and love the people (Arabs) with whom they minister.'

Letters passed to and fro and on the 22nd April 1982 I arrived at Tel Aviv Airport to be met by Alex Awad and his daughter Christie to spend time at the School and College and to meet and pray with all involved in the ministry. By the end of the week I was settled in my mind that I was to work at Bethlehem Bible College and Hope School and I returned to Bristol to begin preparations for my return to Bethlehem.

The final event was my commissioning by the Reverend Ray Brazier in the presence of the church congregation, my family and friends. The opening sentence chosen was, 'Jesus said, "You did not choose me but I chose you to go and bear fruit – fruit that will last." (John 15:16)

Finally, on 29th June I boarded the coach, the first stage of my journey, to the Holy Land, destination Bethlehem, this time not just to visit but to stay and 'Feed His Lambs' – the lambs which still hadn't been revealed to me!
Little did I know that my sojourn in the Bethlehem area would last for many years, I finally said farewell Bethlehem in the year 1995. It was only in looking back on those years that I saw the picture that God had already seen for my life when He called me to leave my homeland and family and go . . .
Now I would like to share some of the good times, the difficult times, the happy times that I experienced as I learned to live side by side with the Palestinian Christians whose home Bethlehem was and is.

I arrived at Luton Airport on 1st July 1982 in good time for check-in and waited in the departure lounge to board the plane at 11 am. I was still in the departure lounge to board the plane at 5 pm – the best laid plans of men often go awry – but finally arrived at Tel Aviv Airport just after midnight. My only option was to find a willing taxi driver to take me to Bethlehem; that bit was easy. The problem arose when we arrived, how to find Hope School or the Bible College in the pitch black night at 2 am in the morning. We got hopelessly lost and finally ended up at the Police Station in Manger Square. The friendly Border Policeman picked up my suitcase and accompanied me to a little hotel at the side of the Church of the Nativity. It was called the Palace Hotel. The proprietor opened the door, welcomed me and gave me an en suite bedroom.

I found out I was the only guest in the hotel when I came down for breakfast but I was served a lovely meal and then a telephone call was made on my behalf and Solomon Douhne, Headmaster of Hope School, arrived to take me up the hill to Beit Jala. I had finally arrived.

The immediate problem that appeared on my arrival was where I was going to live! The School Board, who ran the school, felt it was not fitting in an Arabic culture for a single lady to have a room in the school building where there were 50 boarding boys in residence, plus the house fathers.

Although there was room at the Bible College, in Bethlehem at that time there were no solar panels, hence no hot water, so it was finally decided that Monday to Thursday I would share the home of the school Headmaster and his family and work at Hope

School. And Friday and Saturday I would stay with Alex Awad (Acting President) and his wife Brenda and their two children in Beit Sahour and work at the Bible College. I also spent Saturday night and Sunday with them. This arrangement continued for four months when I moved into my own small apartment which was part of the Church of God in Beit Jala.

As I began to settle in and be accepted, not only by the Palestinian Christians but the ex-pat workers and volunteers who had also been led by God to the Bethlehem area, I finally found the lambs I had been called to feed – three flocks in all:

1. The students, especially the boarding boys at Hope School, Beit Jala.
2. The teenage girls who attended the Sunday School at the Church of God in Beit Jala on a Friday afternoon, and also the children of several nationalities who attended the Sunday morning service at the Church of God on the Mount of Olives in Jerusalem.
3. The Palestinian ladies who attended the Church of God Bible Study on a Tuesday afternoon.

I served at Hope School for ten years and in 1992 I took a Sabbatical to write my first book, 'Who from our Mothers' Arms' (Bristol to Bethlehem). As I daily had my quiet time with the Lord I began to pick up scriptures about writing – 'Write a scroll what you see and send it to the churches' Revelation 1 verse 10. 'Go now, write it on a tablet for them, note it in a book that for days to come it may be an everlasting witness' Isaiah 30 verse 18. Also on my visits back to England as I shared about the Bible College and Hope School, people I didn't know came up to me and said, 'You must write a book.'

Obviously that book is not solely about the town of Bethlehem, as this one is, but I would like now to share some of the incidents from it just about Bethlehem.

Needless to say, the mention of the town of Bethlehem immediately makes people think of Christmas and the Nativity and so Chapter 14 of the book is entitled, 'Christmas in Bethlehem', the timescale for this chapter being 1982 to 1992. And I began the chapter as follows –

Before I lived in Bethlehem, Christmas Eve in the Church of England was special to me. I thought of Mary and Joseph, the donkey, the inn, the birth of baby Jesus. I didn't dwell on the long journey Mary and Joseph had been forced to make for the census being taken; the fact they had to beg for accommodation, that the town would be full of soldiers nor even the fact that King Herod, soon after Jesus' birth, would order the killing of all little boys aged from birth to two years in the area. My western mind dwelt on the 'nice' things that happened that first Christmas. The reality of it all didn't sink in, although I always had a sense of wonder and awe as I read and listened to the story.

Yes, there was reality in Bethlehem 2000 years ago, but there was also wonder, awe, worship and adoration of the shepherds and wise men. At Christmastime in Bethlehem in the 20th/21st century there is a definite reality but also still awe, wonder and worship and adoration. Let me share some extracts from Christmas newsletters written whilst I was living there.

1982

We have experienced heavy rain which lasted four days and was very cold so it gave me a foretaste of things to come and made me realise that the carol, 'IN THE BLEAK MIDWINTER FROSTY WIND MADE MOAN' is not out of keeping because Bethlehem in December can be bleak, especially when the cold east wind blows.

I experienced my first fall of snow in Bethlehem on New Year's Day and sharing about that was my answer to friends who wrote in their Christmas cards that first year, 'Aren't you lucky to be spending Christmas in Bethlehem in the sunshine?' !!

1983

I will be in Bethlehem on Christmas Eve to celebrate at the Programme of Christmas Light at Bethlehem Bible College which is situated halfway between Manger Square and the Shepherds Fields. Christians, Pilgrims and Tourists to Bethlehem from all over the world will gather at the Bible College to worship and celebrate Christmas Eve. It will be a little different in Manger Square with checkpoint soldiers and the need for a ticket to get in to the church of the Nativity. However there will be choirs from around the world singing Christmas songs in the square.

1985

This year one special choir will join the choirs gathered in Manger Square on Christmas Eve, the choir from Bethlehem Bible College. A very special occasion for me to see and hear students from the College, dressed in Palestinian traditional costumes and singing in Arabic. For the students themselves, most of whom born in Bethlehem, a wonderful honour to be able to sing worship songs to their Lord and Saviour in His birth place.

1986

Ring out those bells tonight
Bethlehem, Bethlehem,
Follow that star tonight
Bethlehem, Bethlehem

After four years I still get a thrill when I hear the bells of Bethlehem ringing. The bells of the Church of the Nativity are the joyous ones that thrill my heart the most as they ring out the good news that Jesus Christ is born.

The programme this Christmas for the children at the Church of God on the Mount of Olives in Jerusalem, where I led the Sunday School, was somehow very special this year. We presented the Christmas story in mime then sang a medley of Christmas songs and ended by lighting a candle on a birthday cake for Jesus which had been made by Handels Bakery in Bethlehem.

1987

Sadly the celebrations in Manger Square could no longer be held after the Intifada started early in December.

1988

O little town of Bethlehem
How still we see thee lie . . .

The streets of Bethlehem are still and silent today, a forced situation of strikes and curfews on this first anniversary of the Intifada. The town is busy from 9 am to noon when people go about their business and housewives hurriedly buy food for their families. There will be no Christmas celebrations this year for the people of Bethlehem. No celebration in Bethlehem Bible College on Christmas Eve when Palestinian and Jewish believers usually meet together to worship Jesus.

There are hopeful signs – Hope School may open on the 11th December; my work permit is being considered and so it would seem that for the time being my star is still shining over Bethlehem. Please remember us all in Bethlehem this Christmas Eve and please pray for us.

1989

Sadly I haven't found my way to Bethlehem too many times this year, because of the continuing situation.

The saying, 'No news is good news' is often true, but I am sorry to say it is not so of the situation here. Many of you write that you are not getting reports and so feel things are better. They are not and I would ask you to continue to pray for the staff of Hope School, the Bethlehem Bible College and the people of Bethlehem themselves.

1991

No visits to Bethlehem this Christmas for me or my Palestinian Christian friends and neighbours who stayed in the security of their homes to celebrate the birth of our Lord Jesus Christ.

We all longed for the words of the Arabic carol to become reality:

In the evening of Christmas is gone the hatred
In the evening of Christmas is blossoming the earth
In the evening of Christmas is obliterated the war
In the evening of Christmas is flowing the love
When we give the thirsty one a glass (of water)
We have Christmas

When we put on the naked a robe of love we'll have Christmas
When we wipe out the tears in the eyes (of the sad) we'll have
Christmas
When we fill in the heart's hope we'll have Christmas
When we kiss our friend without grudge it will be Christmas
When dies the spirit of revenge it will be Christmas
When extracted from my heart the enemy it will be Christmas
When melts my soul in the person of God
IT WILL BE CHRISTMAS

1992 – 1994

MY SABBATICAL AND RETURN TO BETHLEHEM

Although I intended to take a year out to write my book, for
various reasons it turned out to be 18 months before I eventually
returned on 20th January 1994.

However, Bethlehem was never far from my thoughts or, indeed,
actions during that period. I had only been in England for 2
months when I found myself at Gatwick airport waiting to meet
a group of students with their teacher, George Abu Dayeh, from
Hope School, Beit Jala. Hope Christian Trust, based in the UK
and set up after meeting me at the school and Bible College, had
arranged for them to come to Bristol for a few weeks to meet
with young Christians in the area and have fellowship and share
about their life in the Bethlehem area. They were a credit to Hope
School and wonderful ambassadors for the Palestinian people. I
was so proud of them and thanked God for letting me have this
time with them in my country.

After their return I was then able to get on with the book I knew
I had to write 'Who From Our Mothers – (Bristol to Bethlehem),'

an account of my life up to the day I arrived at Hope School and Bethlehem Bible College. From then on the book became an account, not only of my life, but of the Palestinian people living and serving God in that area during very, very difficult times. The book was finally completed on 21st July 1993, my 53rd birthday. Although the book was finished it wasn't yet quite the time to return to Bethlehem. I'm not sure quite how it happened but I found myself booked for a tour of the USA to promote the book. Janet Angle accompanied me. Janet and her husband John are the founders of Hope Christian Trust and I will share more about them later.

Needless to say, when I returned to England many of the books remained in the USA and now in its second edition it has travelled around the world letting people know what life is like for the Palestinian people living in Bethlehem today.

The final reason for my delay in returning to Bethlehem was because I needed to know that it was God Himself who wanted me to return. That assurance came on the Day of Pentecost (known as Whitsuntide in England) 1993. I attended the morning service at St Matthew's Church, Cotham, Bristol and Reverend Ray Brazier preached on John Chapter 21 – the scripture that took me to Bethlehem in the first place with the words, 'Feed My Lambs'. Ray emphasised that Peter had been given a new job description – he was told by Jesus to 'Feed My Lambs' verse 15 and 'Feed My Sheep' verses 16 and 17.

I knew I was to return to Bethlehem but with a new job description. The door was open for me to return to Bethlehem Bible College to 'Feed His Sheep'. I wasn't actually going to be a Shepherdess, oh no, I was going to have a far grander title – Public Relations Co-ordinator. My new job description from the Lord was to serve His children – Palestinian Christians working and studying at the Bible College and His children who came to the College as visitors and volunteers. I contacted Bishara Awad, President of Bethlehem Bible College, to tell him, 'Yes, I would come and work full time at the College.' On January 20th 1994 I returned to Bethlehem, accompanied by Janet Angle from Hope Christian Trust.

This time I was shown immediately to my accommodation on the College campus, now situated in what was the Helen Keller Home for the Blind on the Hebron Road. Imagine my surprise to find a neat, one bedroom apartment had been prepared for me complete with my own bathroom and the smallest bath I had ever seen.

Janet stayed with me until she had made curtains etc. for the apartment, help me get my furniture out of storage and generally settle in. During the evening of the day she left, there was a knock at my door. On opening it I found two of the students there – Ramon and Hanni. They handed me a piece of paper which had been printed on the computer, a scroll around the edges and in the middle it said: LYNN'S APARTMENT. They looked at me and said, 'We expect you are a little sad now your friend has gone but don't worry, we are here, we will look after you. They were my official student welcome to Bethlehem Bible College and look after me they did!

The main part of my job was to run the Guest House and look after the Volunteer Groups that came to help at the College, people from all over the world who didn't want to be part of a tour group but to get alongside the Palestinian Christians in support. One regular guest was Brother Andrew from Open Doors; he wrote the forward for my book, and I'd like to share part of what he wrote –

'Far too many books have been written on the Middle East – its conflicts, its antagonism, its wars, massacres, crusades, religious tensions and hatred. Far too little has been written about people – yes, there is not just religion, politics and military there are people. Jesus moved about people, good and bad, rich and poor. He was their friend, healer, feeder and ultimately their Saviour.

As for myself, I refuse to choose sides. Rather I have chosen for people. For justice. For peace which can only be based on justice. For sharing Jesus with people, ordinary people. This . . . . disarming book by my good friend Lynn Weaver shows how to do just that. Get personally involved, without choosing sides. Just go and find people, get close to them, listen to them – yes, above all else listen. Offer them your heart, your hand and your shoulder for them to cry on. Just be there . . .'

That is exactly what Brother Andrew did and so have all those people, including myself, done over many years. They have come to Bethlehem to stand beside the Palestinian people, the local men, women and children whose home Bethlehem is.

Christmas of 1994 was very different from the one in 1992 which I have described. Because once again, the people were free to go to Manger Square and celebrate on Christmas Eve. Once again the Bethlehem Bible College Choir joined the choirs in the Square, dressed in their Palestinian traditional costumes and singing with joy to the Lord Jesus, whose birth they were celebrating. Little did I know that Christmas Eve that 12 months hence I would no longer be living in Bethlehem, for God was about to do a special thing in my life.

CHRISTMAS 1995
The Bible College always sent out a Christmas Newsletter to those around the world who supported the College and I also sent a personal Christmas letter to family and friends who supported me. I'd like to share extracts from both letters dated December 1995.

BETHLEHEM BIBLE COLLEGE'S NEWSLETTER shared the following: Bethlehem, a City of Good News, has seen many travellers: Jesus the Messiah, the Saviour of the World, came down from heaven to be born here in a lowly manger. King David was also born in Bethlehem and tended his flocks in the fields nearby. Bethlehem, as a city of romance, saw Ruth and Boaz, ancestors of Jesus, engaged and married.
This Christmas another romance has blossomed for one of our faithful staff, Miss Lynn Weaver. After serving the Lord unceasingly in Bethlehem for 12 years, Lynn has become engaged to Malcolm Jones who visited the Bible College as a volunteer with Helps International Ministries of which Malcolm is Director of Europe and the Middle East. We are thankful to Lynn for the love she has shared so freely with the Palestinians of Bethlehem. Our love and congratulations go with Lynn as she returns to England for her December 16th wedding.'

MY PERSONAL NEWSLETTER read:

The Book of Ecclesiastes Chapter 3 says, 'There is a time for everything – a time of change . . .'

This year of 1995 there is a time of change in the City of Bethlehem which, throughout the centuries, has experienced many changes. Yet again it will see another major change for on 13th December the Israeli Army of Occupation is due to withdraw and the Christmas Celebrations in Manger Square will be under the control of the Palestinian Police Force.

I, too, have experienced many changes in my lifetime, the most significant one for me being, of course, my coming to Bethlehem in 1982 to serve the Palestinian Christians. I, too, like Bethlehem will experience another major change this Christmastime as 'my Shepherd' leads me back to my homeland to become the wife of Malcolm Jones. Please pray for us both as we prepare for our wedding day.'

As God brought Ruth to Bethlehem to meet Boaz, so God brought both Malcolm and me to Bethlehem to meet each other. Very briefly, it happened this way –

1 The venue for our first meeting – Bethlehem Bible College.

2 The reason for our meeting – Malcolm, who at the time was Director of Helps International Ministries, Europe and the Middle East, arrived at the College for a few days to be with an HIM Team who had come to the College to rebuild the shower block. I was in charge of the Guest House at the time and so was there to take care of him.

3 This included being Tour Guide, taking the group to Manger Square and the Church of the Nativity. After

lunch at the Christmas Tree Cafe we took the bus to Beit Sahour and walked to the Shepherd's Fields, passing the very fields where Ruth and Boaz met. During the walk I asked Malcolm if he could possibly find a couple who could come to the College, the wife to help me and the man to take care of the maintenance. He said he would do his best.

4 The following day, which was Palm Sunday, we all went to the Garden Tomb in Jerusalem to take part in a recording for the British TV programme of Songs of Praise for Easter. After the service Malcolm and I said goodbye, he to return to England and I back to the Bible College.

5 So began a correspondence between Malcolm and me, primarily to arrange for the couple he had found to come and work at the College. However, when I returned to Bristol in August 1995 for a vacation, I visited Malcolm in his home in Lancashire and when I returned to Bristol and then Bethlehem I shared the news that I had become engaged to be married to him!

6 In November 1995 Malcolm returned to Bethlehem. The President of the Bible College, Dr Bishara Awad, and his wife Salwa arranged an official Palestinian engagement celebration for us. The Chapel of the Bible College was packed for a Service of Blessing in English and Arabic. Some of the ladies from the House of Hope for the Blind and Sister Sheera's Home for the Blind in Beit Jala sang for us. The celebration ended with the cutting of a cake with our names written in icing on the top.

7 It was time for me to say farewell to Bethlehem after 12 years of living and sharing every day ups and downs with

my Palestinian sisters and brothers in Christ. Malcolm and I were married on the 16th December 1995 and I was wearing a beautiful gown, embroidered with gold thread and made for me by the Palestinian Women's Sewing Guild in Beit Jala. Our home in England had lots of reminders of Bethlehem as friends gave us items of embroidery and glassware and pottery made in the area.

BETHLEHEM REVISITED

In September 1996 Malcolm and I, together with four friends, travelled to Bethlehem to be with the staff and students as they celebrated the official handing over ceremony of the Bethlehem Bible College buildings, once the Helen Keller Home for the Blind and owned by the Bible Lands Society based in High Wycombe, England. The Society has now been renamed Embrace and has supported, and continues to support, Palestinians in Bethlehem for many, many years.

Guests from all over the world arrived to join the local Palestinian Christians. Brother Andrew gave the address in English and Alex Awad in Arabic. Gifts were given, made of olive wood, to groups who had contributed to improving the campus in many ways. Helps International Ministries were thanked for the work they had done restoring the building – Malcolm's team in 1993 converted rooms for Bishara Awad (the President) and his family. The result of their labours was a beautiful apartment for Bishara, Salwa and their children Sami, Samir and Dina. In 1994 an HIM team of four – Eric and Gwen Kendall and Ken and Joyce Bird – converted rooms into shower units for the students.

After the official handover we all adjourned to the roof of the third building (where I had had my apartment) and the foundation stone was laid for the new library, guest house and community room.

One morning, during our stay, Malcolm and I walked down to Manger Square. On the way we passed the barber's shop where Malcolm got his hair cut when he was at the college in 1993. The barber was so happy to see him and, of course, I was introduced. So it was, 'Take a seat, have some Arabic coffee and visit!' This invitation was extended several times before we finally reached Manger Square. At the hardware store where I bought my pots and pans, we were served tea with mint and given a wedding gift of a pizza tray.

Then walking into Manger Square we were stopped by the cry of, 'Sister Lynn, Sister Lynn' and, as I turned to see who it was, saw Murfeed who owned a souvenir shop. Murfeed never forgets a face and as soon as he saw me he said, 'Come on in to my shop, what would you like – tea, coffee, juice?' We quickly declined but sat and chatted to him. Then he reached up and took down a beautiful painted plate of Bethlehem and said, 'This is a wedding present from me.'

Finally we ended up at the Christmas Tree Cafe and had lunch – shawarma (lamb meat cooked on a spit, sliced thinly and served in a pitta bread). The owner of the cafe was so pleased to see us and needless to say served us falafel as well without charging us for it.

Arabic hospitality is well known and we had just spent a whole morning with Palestinians who were genuinely pleased to see us and expressed their love in gifts to us.

Our flight back to the UK was on a Sunday evening so in the morning Malcolm and I went to the Bethlehem Baraka Church where we enjoyed fellowship with Pastor Awad and his wife; Sami (the Pastor's son) and his wife Sarah who ran the House of Joy for girls with disabilities; Edward Vollbehr from Beit Jemima, a home for severely handicapped children, and many Palestinian friends.

After the service we received several invitations to share lunch but we had arranged to have lunch with our group at the Mt Everest Hotel – through Beit Jala, past Hope School and high into the Judean hills; a fitting end to our first return to Bethlehem.
Towards the end of 1999 we received a message via John and Janet Angle (Hope Christian Trust) from Bishara and Salwa Awad – 'Please would you come and help us to celebrate the first Greek Orthodox Christmas of the millennium in Bethlehem?' Yes, we would! And on the 5th January 2000 we met John and Janet at Gatwick Airport and once again flew out to Tel Aviv.

Rich and Barbara Banis (the couple who responded to Malcolm's request to come to Bethlehem Bible College and take over the tasks I had carried out there) came to meet us at the airport. It was cold and wet and began to snow a little when we arrived in Bethlehem but when we saw our room in the Bethlehem Inn, the new guest house at the College, we forgot the cold. Churches and groups and individuals from around the world had made donations to furnish each room. Malcolm and I had a room at the back of the building looking up to the top of Mt Everest with the town of Beit Jala in the foreground. I was able to point out to Malcolm where our friends lived plus St Nicholas Church and St Mary's Church and Hope School. However, we both realised that a big change had taken place as we looked at a major highway that now crossed the valley and the settlement of Har Gilo had now extended down the hillside and was very close to the college. The highway which ran from Jerusalem to Hebron was for Israeli citizens to avoid having to come through Bethlehem.

The new guest house had a lovely lounge area, a large kitchen/dining room at the front of the building overlooking the Hebron Road and a small refugee camp. The wall, not too high, in front of the camp is part of the remains of an aqueduct built by King Hezekiah to bring water from Solomon's Pools to Jerusalem.

The changes at the college were the first of many we were to see as we walked through Bethlehem the following day which was the Christmas Eve for the Greek Orthodox. The area in the vicinity of Manger Square had been transformed with new buildings with financial aid from overseas, mostly from Scandinavian countries.

Manger Square was a different place, no cars or tourist buses allowed to park there anymore. There was new paving and the cafes, on the left hand side of the Square, had gone including our favourite, The Christmas Tree Cafe. We eventually found it on the road going out of Bethlehem to Jerusalem. In their place an Information Bureau and an Institute for Peace had been built. There was also a new atmosphere, no more soldiers or tanks and jeeps. Instead, Palestinian police patrolled the area.

IT WAS CHRISTMAS EVE.
IT WAS MILLENNIUM and
THERE WAS FREEDOM TO CELEBRATE.

The traditional stage for the choirs to sing was in place but instead of standing room only, rows of chairs were in place and there was no army checkpoint to go through to get into the Square.

We found a seat and sat down to enjoy the choirs. The two choirs that stay in my memory were the Bible College Choir and a Russian Choir. The Russian Choir sang many songs with individuals and groups performing. They sang in Russian but the words were translated into English and every song was about the Lord Jesus and the faces of the singers shone.

For me, it was so special when the Bible College Choir sang. The purpose of the college is 'to keep the light of Christ shining in the little town of His birth.' The choir are indeed a light that shines.

On our last day at the Bible College Janet and I stayed in to pack for our journey back home. John and Malcolm decided to make a quick trip to Hebron. On their return Malcolm walked into our room, told me to close my eyes and hold my hands out. He then placed something soft and warm into them. It was a goat skin rug. We had looked all over the place for one but for some reason nobody had one. John had taken Malcolm down a side street in Hebron, close to the cave of Machpelah which Abraham bought for a place to bury Sarah. As they walked they saw a little shop selling rugs and went in. Malcolm said there was a whole pile of goat skin rugs so he went through the pile until he found one he liked. The rug went into the suitcase and travelled back to England with us – a tangible reminder of Bethlehem revisited.

'LET US NOW GO TO BETHLEHEM AND SEE THIS THING THAT HAS COME TO PASS WHICH THE LORD HAS MADE KNOWN TO US.'

So said the Shepherds after they had experienced the Glory of the Lord and been told that unto them, in the City of David, a Saviour had been born.

The scene where they were watching their sheep had returned to normal. The night sky full of stars, their homes in the hamlet of Beit Sahour (The House of the Shepherds) in darkness as their families slept.

They lifted their eyes to see the winding path up to the little town of Bethlehem and began to climb the hill and the Bible tells us: 'THEY CAME AND FOUND MARY AND JOSEPH AND THE BABE, LYING IN A MANGER.'

Let us lift our eyes to see and to find the comings and goings of mankind from the time of the Shepherds until our own moment of time in the year 2018.

Bethlehem lies five miles south of Jerusalem on a hill about 2600 feet above sea level. From the hill the town looks across to the Dead Sea. The land surrounding Bethlehem is very fertile.

Known as David's City it is said that David and his family neglected their city, which became obscure, forgotten by all except those who looked to Bethlehem for the Messiah.

The city again became important as the birthplace of Jesus.

In AD 135 Hadrian desecrated the traditional place of the nativity with a grove sacred to Adonis.

In AD 315 Constantine destroyed the heathen grove and constructed instead the Church of the Nativity which was completed in AD 333.

The city was sacked by the Samaritans in AD 529 but was rebuilt by the Byzantine emperor Justinian I.

In AD 637 Bethlehem was conquered by the Arab Caliphate of Umar ibn al-Khattab, who guaranteed safety for the religious shrines.

In 1099 the Crusaders captured and fortified Bethlehem and replaced its Greek Orthodox clergy with a Latin one.

The Latin clergy were expelled after the city was captured by Saladin the Sultan of Egypt and Syria.

With the coming of the Mamluks in 1250 the city walls were demolished and were subsequently rebuilt during the rule of the Ottoman Empire, who annexed the city in 1571 AD.

With the fall of the Ottoman Empire, Bethlehem became part of the British administered Palestinian Mandate from 1922 until 1948 when it joined Jordan.

After the 1967 Arab-Israeli War, Bethlehem became part of the Israeli-occupied territories, administered militarily by Israeli troops. Palestinian refugee camps were located nearby.

In December 1995, Israeli troops withdrew from Bethlehem as part of the process of establishing Palestinian self-rule in the West Bank. However, the city was the scene of Palestinian-Israeli fighting in the renewed conflict that began in 2000.

History is important but far more important are the people who have inhabited the town down the centuries. I have many happy memories of sitting under fig trees drinking Arabic coffee and sharing with my hosts the stories of their families handed down from generation to generation. I wish now I had written them down but I can share about the Palestinians who live in the town today, their way of life, their occupations, their customs . . . so I will make myself a cup of Arabic coffee, with cardamom of course, and remember the people and the town where I lived for 12 years.

The town is inhabited by one of the oldest Christian communities in the world, though the size of the community has shrunk in recent years due to emigration.

Modern Bethlehem has a Muslim majority but has the largest Palestinian Christian community in the Holy Land. As I have already said, Bethlehem is part of the Christian Triangle which included Beit Jala and Beit Sahour and includes the Refugee Camps of Aida and Azza and the large camp called Deheishe which are inhabited by the Muslim community.

Although the Israeli occupation ended in 1995 Israel has retained control over the entrances and exits to Bethlehem but the day to day administration is overseen by the Palestinian National

Authority.

The inhabitants of Bethlehem depend largely on pilgrims and tourists for their livelihood, particularly during the Christmas season when pilgrims flock to Manger Square to visit the Church of the Nativity, the birthplace of Jesus.

The skilled craftsmen have their workshops in the town and outlying villages and you can stand and watch them carving olive wood nativity sets, camels, donkeys and beautiful filigree Christmas tree ornaments as well as other carvings. I have a beautiful carving of Jesus as a boy at his carpenter's bench; Jesus washing His disciples' feet and Jesus the Good Shepherd. I also have a beautiful vase depicting the Nativity Scene and the Star of Bethlehem, plus camels in various poses and a donkey too.

One of my tasks at Bethlehem Bible College was to run the souvenir shop where groups visiting the College could buy their souvenirs. I obtained my olive wood carvings from two sources. The first was Abu Basem and his son Basem who lived in Beit Jala and carved camels and donkeys. When an Arabic couple have their firstborn son they become known by their son's name, for example Abu Basem, the father of Basem and Imm Basem, the mother of Basem. The first names of my Abu and Imm Basem are Naim and Jeanette and their surname is el Yeteem. They were in fact my landlord and landlady as I lived in a small apartment in the building of the Church of God in Beit Jala, which was owned by them.

My second supplier, Issa Musleh, organised a co-operative in which local workers in olive wood, mother of pearl and other crafts displayed and sold their work. Since 1995 two volunteers who worked alongside me at the Bible College, Frederick and Laura Ann Zahn, on their return to the USA have organised sales of olive wood purchased from Issa and have used the profits to support several Christian Palestinian ministries.

The tradition of making handicrafts in the city goes back to its founding. Numerous shops in Bethlehem sell olive wood carvings for which the city is renowned. The carvings are the main product purchased by tourists visiting Bethlehem.

Religious handicrafts are also a major industry and so products include ornaments and jewellery made from the Mother of Pearl. This art was introduced to Bethlehem by Franciscan friars from Damascus during the 14th century. Other religious items of olive wood are statues, boxes and crosses.

Stone and marble-cutting, textiles, furniture and furnishings are other prevalent industries. Bethlehem also produces paints, plastics, synthetic rubber, pharmaceuticals, construction materials and food products, mainly pasta and confectionary.

The latter brings back some enjoyable memories for me as in my mind's eye I can see the confectionary shop of Handels and the display of luscious gateaux cream cakes and chocolate éclairs. We didn't need to wait for a celebration to go to Handels and bring the cakes back and enjoy them with a cup of Arabic coffee. Just next to the Bible College was another Arabic sweetmeats shop selling baklava, hareesa (a sponge cake with almonds and syrup) and lots of other sweet and sticky delights.

Bethlehem also has a wine producing company, Cremisan Wine

founded in 1885, that currently exports wine to several countries. The wine is produced by monks in the Monastery of Cremisan and the majority of the grapes are harvested from the al-Khader (St George) area on the way to Hebron. The monastery's wine production is around 700,000 litres per year.

A visit Malcolm and I made to the monks at Cremisan brings back yet another happy memory. It was a warm, sunny day and we were staying at the guest house at Bethlehem Bible College. I wanted to take some wine home to give to my family as a Christmas gift. It is not too often you can have a glass of wine from Bethlehem with your Christmas lunch! The monastery is situated near the top of Mt Everest near to Hope School in Beit Jala. We climbed the hill, turned off onto a path on the right which led us down into the valley. We rang the bell outside the little shop and waited and waited. Finally, one of the monks arrived and took us inside. He proceeded to suggest different wines we might like and of course each one had to be tried – just a sip from Malcolm and me but we noticed the monk drank all that was in his glass. We finally made our purchase and a happy, smiling monk waved us on our way. It had been a very pleasant trip especially as it brought back another happy memory for me.

One lovely Friday afternoon I decided to take my Girls Class (the Nade Shabaat), which I ran at the Church of God in Beit Jala, for a picnic in the valley by the monastery. About 15 teenage girls, my translator Claude Abu Dayeh and I set off up the hill. The girls didn't get many outings so they were so excited and we all enjoyed ourselves amongst the olive trees and grape vines and sat on warm rocks to enjoy the food we had brought. Sadly that wouldn't be possible today as the highway from Jerusalem to Hebron, built in order to bypass Bethlehem, runs right across the valley.

During our stay at the Bible College Malcolm and I went for a walk along the main Hebron Road. A little further along the road from the College we came across a building site. Malcolm immediately stopped; he could never resist watching builders at work, that being his trade. The building had reached the flat roof level and the workers on the roof immediately called us to go up the ladder to talk to them. The building was going to be a factory for making socks; the money had been donated from Sweden. That was good news for the workmen and down the line for those who would be given a job in the factory.

Finding work in Bethlehem was and still is very hard. One of the workers recognised me as he lived near Hope School and before we knew it a makeshift bench had been made for us to sit down and then a young man climbed up the ladder with the midday meal and we were given a can of orange and paper plates of pitta bread, hummus and falafel. The builder who recognised me said he would have liked to ask us to his home for a proper meal but they were working non-stop to complete the building by the deadline date. To me that was yet again an example of the countless number of times I had been invited to share a coffee or fruit or cake and many, many full meals in the homes of my Palestinian friends, neighbours and even strangers. Hospitality is the lynch pin of Arabic culture.

I could write a whole book on the hospitality I was given during my 12 years sojourn in Bethlehem but there is one that I simply must share . . .

MY VISIT TO THE DEHEISHE REFUGEE CAMP

Imm Mustafa, one of the ladies who cleaned at the school, would bring me bread and little pasties with spinach inside as well as toot (mulberries), figs and grapes. She lived in the Deheishe Refugee Camp with her family and although she spoke no English and my Arabic was limited, we grew to love each other very much. She kept asking me to go to her home and finally I agreed, in spite of my neighbours telling me it wasn't safe to go alone to the Refugee Camp. 'I'm not going alone, I'm going with Imm Mustafa,' was my response. So one day after school I walked along the road with her to get the bus to her home.

It was my first visit to a Refugee Camp and as we entered I noticed the open sewer running down the narrow lanes between the small houses; houses with just two rooms for the families who lived there; families who had all been turned out of their own houses in the villages in 1948 and who were still living in these dwelling places provided by the United Nations.

When I arrived at Imm Mustafa's house I was pleasantly surprised. It was at the end of a row and so had more space and even a little garden with a grape vine and flowers. There was even a little brick building where the food was prepared and cooked. Imm Mustafa's second son, Mohammad, was home and one of her daughters. They both spoke English and Mohammad's friend, who joined us later also spoke good English so I was able to relax and enjoy the visit.

I was served in the normal Arabic way. First a glass of orange juice, then a bowl of fruit was brought in and I was given a plate which had grapes, an apple and a banana on it. In time I came to learn I didn't have to eat them all. It was quite acceptable if I just ate one piece of fruit. Finally, I was served the black Arabic coffee, after which it is in order to leave, the visit being over. So on this occasion, after the coffee, I rose to leave but was immediately told to sit down as supper was being prepared for me. What a supper!

Imm Mustafa appeared carrying a very large round metal tray piled high with rice and chicken. Her daughter came in with a pot of soup made from the chicken stock, with potatoes and parsley in it. Then appeared olives, bread, salad, plus a jug of goat's yogurt, the texture of milk. The latter I had to decline as the acrid taste as it hit the back of my throat, plus the smell, brought tears to my eyes. The rest of the meal I was able to enjoy and after eating my fill and being given a towel to wipe my hands on (most of the meal had been eaten with my fingers) I felt this time I could rise and take my leave.

Mohammad and his friend said they would escort me to the main road to get a taxi and as I came out of the room into the yard Imm Mustafa came from her kitchen with a bag of fresh round flat bread for me. She then proceeded to cut a huge bunch of grapes from the small garden and placed them all in my arms. I turned to her daughter and said, 'Why is she giving me all this?' The daughter looked at me surprised and said, 'My mother loves you.' The young men walked me through the camp squalor to the main gate. Mohammad hailed a taxi, his friend opened the door for me to get in and then Mohammad said, 'I have told the taxi to take you to your home and I have paid him the fare.' As the taxi drew away tears flowed down my cheeks. Here was I, my arms full of bread, fruit and flowers, my heart full of love bestowed on me by this Muslim family and there stood these two young men, smiling and waving goodbye before turning to return to their home; a home in a refugee camp surrounded by barbed wire (later the wire was replaced by corrugated tin panels) and a home that was constantly put under curfew which meant the family had to stay inside the two rooms, sometimes for weeks at a time, with no electricity or water until the curfew was lifted allowing them out for a short while to get food supplies from the United Nations food store; a home that would later bear bullet holes in the walls from soldiers shooting into the house and narrowly missing Mohammad's baby daughter's cot.

For Mohammad later married and I was present at the wedding celebrations when he brought his wife to his home. (He had been to the bride's home, riding on a white horse to collect his bride from her family). Their baby daughter, when she was born, was given the name Rosleen, a name very similar to the name I was given at my birth – Rosalind.
This family was used by the Lord to bless me abundantly and will always have a place in my heart.

One of the other memories of Imm Mustafa is the day she arrived at Hope School and handed me a plastic bag and inside I found a traditional Arabic dress of the Bethlehem area. It was made of black material and embroidered at the neck in red cross stitch. She then took out a large muslin square and told me to go and put them on. I managed the dress but didn't quite know what to do with the muslin, although I knew it had to go on my head! So I gave it to Imm Mustafa who put it firmly in place and then took a photograph of me. I never did find out what the procedure was all about.

That incident reminds me of the importance of the beautiful costumes and embroidery that are a part of the Bethlehem culture.

Before the establishment of Israel as a state, Bethlehem costumes and embroidery were popular in villages throughout the Judean Hills and the coastal plain. The women embroiderers of Bethlehem and the neighbouring villages of Beit Jala and Beit Sahour were known to be professional producers of wedding costumes. Bethlehem was a centre for embroidery producing a 'strong overall effect of colours and metallic brilliance.' (The only problem I had with the ladies at Beit Jala who made my wedding dress was because I just wanted gold embroidery. At each fitting the lady making the dress kept saying, 'Let me add a little green and a little red.' My reply was always the same, 'La-a bass dahab. No, just gold!' And gold it was.)

Less formal dresses in Bethlehem were generally made of indigo fabric, and a sleeveless coat (bisht), made from locally woven wool, was worn over the top. Dresses for special occasions were made of striped silk with winged sleeves and the short taqsireh jacket, known throughout Palestine as the Bethlehem jacket, was worn over it. The taqsireh was made of velvet or broadcloth, usually with heavy embroidery.

Bethlehem work was unique in its use of couched gold and silver cord onto the silk, wool, felt or velvet used for the garment, to create stylized floral patterns with free or rounded lines. (This was the embroidery on my wedding dress with a large area of embroidery at the neck, round the sleeve edges and around the slits at the bottom of the dress. The seamstress also made a small Juliette cap (like a skull cap) and embroidered around the rim. The material for the dress and cap was off-white in colour, one side being shiny and the other plain, the embroidery being done on the plain side. This technique was used for 'royal' wedding dresses (thob malak), taqsirehs and the shatwehs worn by married women. It has been traced by some to Byzantium and the others to more formal costumes of the Ottoman Empire's elite.

As Bethlehem was a Christian village, local women were also exposed to the detailing on church vestments with their heavy embroidery and silver brocades.

Bethlehem is home to the Palestinian Heritage Centre, established in 1991. The centre aims to preserve and promote Palestinian embroidery, art and folklore.

The International Centre of Bethlehem is another cultural centre that concentrates primarily on the culture of Bethlehem. It provides language and guide training, women's studies and arts and crafts displays and training.

During my time in Bethlehem I got to know some of the ladies who are continuing the traditions in embroidery handed down to them through the years and I looked forward to the sales of work they held from time to time and was able to buy some beautiful gifts for my family and friends.

Life today in Bethlehem is not easy, with so many restrictions that hinder everyday living. It wasn't easy for me during the 12 years I lived there but I will never forget the impact my Palestinian neighbours, friends and colleagues had on me for, in spite of the difficulties, they strove to live their lives in their traditions and always seemed ready with a smile and laughter and were kind to me, a stranger in their land.

BETHLEHEM 2019

For many communities around the world everyday living is very difficult and as we watch the scenes on the television screens our hearts go out to the people involved. However, it is mostly the crisis situations that make us aware of what is going on around the word, then the crisis is over and fresh news takes its place, so we no longer hear of the daily life that has to continue post-crisis.

In this next section I want to share what everyday life, right now, is like for the Palestinians living in the town of Bethlehem.

For me, personally, I know this section will be very emotional. For you who read it I pray it will give you empathy and understanding of the people who call Bethlehem home. They are the Christians, who not only live alongside their Muslim neighbours, but who continue to lift up the name of Jesus at Christmastime, and every day, and in so doing are keeping the light of Christ shining in the town of His birth.

FIRST A FEW STATISTICS ABOUT BETHLEHEM
GOVERNMENT
Bethlehem is the (muhfaza) seat or district capital of the Bethlehem Governorate. The Bethlehem Municipal Council consists of fifteen elected members, including the mayor and deputy mayor. A special statute requires that the mayor and a majority of the municipal council must be Christian, while the remainder are open seats, not restricted to any religion.

EDUCATION
Education is highly valued by the Palestinians and all try to get

their children into Primary, Secondary and High School.

In 2006 there were 135 schools in the Bethlehem Governorate, 100 of these being run by the Education Ministry of the Palestinian national Authority, and 7 by the United Nations Relief and Works Agency (UNRWA). These schools would be in the Refugee Camps – Dehaisha-Aida-Azza.

Bethlehem is home to Bethlehem University, a Catholic Christian co-educational institution of higher learning founded in 1973 in the Lasallian tradition open to students of all faiths. Bethlehem University is the first university established in the West Bank and can trace its roots to 1893 when the De La Salle Christian Brothers opened schools throughout Palestine and Egypt.

Hope School, Beit Jala, where I worked for 10 years was started by the Mennonites from the USA and handed over to be run by a board of local residents. Bishara Awad became the first Palestinian Principal and in time Bishara became the Principal of Bethlehem Bible College, supported by his lovely wife Salwa; but more about that later.

Just up the road, at the top of Mt Everest, Beit Jala, is the Talitha Cumi School, run by the Lutheran Church.

Many of the schools in the area are operated by Christian organisations and maintained by sponsorship from people all over the world. Today there is the American School in Beit Jala and a Swedish school, both for local children.

MOVEMENT RESTRICTION

The Israeli construction of the West Bank barrier (a very high concrete wall with watchtowers) has had an impact on Bethlehem politically, socially and economically.

The barrier runs along the northern side of the town's built-up area within metres of houses in Aida Refugee Camp on one side and the Jerusalem municipality on the other.

Most entrances and exits from Bethlehem area to the rest of the West Bank are subject to Israeli checkpoints and roadblocks. The level of access varies based on Israeli security directives.

Travel for Bethlehem's Palestinian residents from the West Bank into the Israel-annexed Jerusalem is regulated by a permit system. Acquiring such permits to enter is a time-consuming and lengthy occupation. I remember during my time the hours I spent trying to obtain a work permit, standing in line in the hot sun, the people behind pushing to move you forward and then once inside the building sitting for hours on a stone bench and sometimes not even seeing anyone to sign my papers. However, my British passport sometimes helped me to gain access but for the Palestinians the queuing could begin very early in the morning until around 3 o'clock in the afternoon, and not even being able to gain access to the inside of the building. When I first arrived and heard my neighbours saying they were 'working' on their papers I thought it strange until I began the process myself.

Of course the West Bank barrier or 'Wall' hadn't been constructed when I lived there, my last visit to Bethlehem being in 2000. There was of course the Checkpoint as you left Bethlehem to join the road to Jerusalem. This was an open checkpoint with a watchtower in the middle of the road – you were checked on the way out and again on your way back in. My British passport assured me of a hassle-free passage, not so the Palestinians who were on the bus or in the taxi with me, and I witnessed many disturbing incidents, especially to the young men who were trying to get into Jerusalem to find work.

Now, however, it is much harder to get in and out of Bethlehem. I had only heard my friends, who visit Bethlehem regularly, describe the procedure and it was only when I saw the checkpoint on the television that I realised the reality that faced Bethlehem's residents on a daily basis as they sought to go to Jerusalem in order to find work, to obtain medical care, to visit the holy places and members of families. My heart sank as I saw the vastness of the towering wall which surrounds Bethlehem and the checkpoint itself which involves negotiating turnstiles, tunnel-like walkways and an area where permits, passports and paperwork have to be shown before you can either leave or enter Bethlehem and always fear in your heart of being told to go back – either to Bethlehem or Jerusalem.

When Malcolm and I had our engagement celebrations in 1995 at Bethlehem Bible College none of the above hurdles existed, yet as we chatted with our guests and Malcolm asked one of them what life was like for her living in Bethlehem I have never forgotten her answer, 'We are living in a cage. Yes, we are free to live our normal lives inside the cage but it is difficult to get out of the cage.' The 'cage' wasn't tangible then; now in 2018 the 'cage' consists of a solid concrete wall many metres high surrounding the city and the gateway is like an assault course which is manned by armed soldiers.

One positive aspect of it all is that tour buses are allowed to go through the checkpoint without difficulty and that means that once inside the city tourists can visit the Biblical sites, buying handcrafted souvenirs, visit restaurants and see the local residents going about their daily life. What the tourist probably doesn't realise is that by being there they are showing the Palestinian people that they care, that people from around the world have come to visit their city and that they are not alone in their 'cage'.

STEADFAST HOPE

It is good to note that Bethlehem has at least 43 'sister' cities around the world, 13 of them being in Italy.

Many countries also help the city with financial aid, either individual nations or via the United Nations thus providing help for education, medical help and the provision of food supplies, especially for those who, because of the situation, are unable to help themselves.

As well as this aid many individuals from around the world volunteer to help in all sorts of ways showing the people that they are not standing alone in their very difficult day by day living.

Furthermore, there are many Palestinians born and raised in the area who are involved in working to help their home city of Bethlehem in all spheres of 'social' help e.g. Education (homes for the blind and handicapped) – Schools – Welfare etc, some having studied in other countries and returned to share their expertise and some who have never left.

In this section of this Anthology I would like to share just some of these ministries in more detail, though I realise there are many unsung ministries who daily continue to help the Palestinian people of Bethlehem today.

It seems right I should begin by sharing about the two indigenous ministries that I worked alongside during my 12 years sojourn in Bethlehem.

HOPE SECONDARY SCHOOL
AL AMAL in ARABIC
(Amal meaning Hope)

Situated on the top of one of the highest hills in Judea, overlooking Bethlehem.

The buildings were originally built as a hospital but never used for that purpose and the family who owned them gave them to the Orthodox Charitable Society of Beit Jala to be used for the benefit of the town.

In 1962 the buildings were leased to the Mennonite Central Committee (U.S.A.) who started a school for boys aged 12 years upwards. Most of the students were boarding students but some came daily. The Mennonite Central Committee ran the school until 1971 when they decided to hand it over to the local Palestinians living in Beit Jala and the Bethlehem area.

Bishara Awad, who had been raised in Jerusalem and Bethlehem and then gone to the U.S.A. to study, decided to return to the West Bank and became the first Palestinian Principal of the school. He formed a Charitable Society to oversee the running of the School. This meant the School would have to become totally self-supporting as the Mennonite Central Committee gradually withdrew. Not an easy undertaking but Bishara, together with his wife Salwa and family Sammy, Samir and Dina, devoted the next 11 years to caring for the students at the School. Some were orphans, many with only one parent and the majority from poor homes.

Bishara's own background had given him a strong desire to help these boys. In Bishara's own words, 'At the tender age of 9, in 1948, I watched as my father was shot in front of our house.' Bishara's family lived near Damascus Gate in Jerusalem. One evening, they heard shooting outside and his father, who was the Red Cross man in the area, waited a while for it to quieten then went out to see if his help was needed. He forgot to put on his Red Cross identification; there was one more shot and his father was killed. Bishara helped his mother to bury his father in the garden as the whole area was under curfew. A short while later they were turned out of their home and Bishara said, 'Hatred mushroomed into bitterness inside me.' He and six brothers and sisters were put into an orphanage and his mother, Huda, returned to nursing in order to support her family. However, when he became a young man he had a life-changing encounter with Jesus Christ and all the bitterness and hatred changed. This put a new perspective into his life and he decided to pour his life into bringing God's love into the lives of his own people.

As he looked at the boys of Hope School, many in the same position as he had been in, he didn't want them to grow up with hatred and bitterness in their hearts and he dedicated his life to sharing God's love with them.

In 1981 Bishara decided to relinquish the Principal's position though he remained on the School Board and continued a care and concern for the school. He became President of Bethlehem Bible College, more about that later.

I arrived at Hope School in 1982 and the Reverend Solomon

Douhne had been appointed Principal. Solomon's own mother had died when he was a little boy in Syria. At sixteen years old and with little education he came into contact with a minister of a church in Darra. The minister, who was blind, had been forced to leave his Palestine homeland several years earlier. Solomon got on well with the minister and was able to lead him around the town on his visits to people. It was through this pastor that Solomon got work in an orphanage in Beirut and then went on to the Church of God Bible College, first in Switzerland and then at Lee College, U.S.A. He settled in the U.S.A and married Sue, who he met at Lee College, and they both became teachers and had three children – David and twins Stephen and Stephanie. Then Solomon began to have a distinct urge to return to the Middle East. He had met and formed a strong bond of friendship with Alex Awad, Bishara's brother, and so Alex, who was teaching at Hope School then, suggested that Solomon be asked to become Principal of the School and Solomon accepted the invitation.

Also at the school when I arrived was the Arabic Secretary, George Shawrieh. George, to me, is a shining example of all that Hope School and Bethlehem Bible College stand for. He himself had been a student at Hope School. His father was unable to work and his mother had to bear the load of providing for her six children. George and his two brothers, Odeh and Roni, came to the school and also their sister Nuha came as a day student. On his graduation George went to study at Bethlehem Bible College and then received a scholarship for one year to Christ For The Nations Bible College in Dallas, Texas. At the end of this year Hope School needed an Arabic Secretary and George was asked to consider this.

Life in the U.S.A. for a young Palestinian man was very different from his life in the occupied West Bank and it was a big temptation for George to stay in the U.S.A. However, George decided to pray about it and finally telephoned to say he would return and accept the post because he knew the Lord wanted him to serve his own people.

Romans 5 verse 5 tells us:

'And hope does not disappoint us, because God has poured out his love into our hearts by the Holy Spirit, whom he has given us.'

That, to me, is what the ministry of Hope School was all about. God had placed His love in our hearts and through His Holy Spirit enabled us to pass on His love to the boys and girls whom He placed into our care. For Hope School was, and still is, more than a place of learning. It was home to 50+ boarding students and for all the students, day and boarding, boys and girls, it was a place where they heard the good news that Jesus Christ died for each one of them.

My job as Sponsorship Secretary was to prepare a case history for each student which I sent to sponsors around the world. In the ten years I was at the school the Sponsorship Scheme expanded from the Mennonite Central Committee U.S.A., the Bible Lands Society (now renamed Embrace) UK and World Vision to include individual sponsorship from Friends of Hope School in England (now Hope Christian Trust) and sponsors in the U.S.A., Canada, Iceland, Sweden, Germany, Holland, Australia and New Zealand.

George Shawrieh remained as the Arabic Secretary, as I did as English Secretary, but we had three changes of Principal.

Solomon Douhne returned to the U.S.A. and Issam Hessen (a graduate of Bethlehem Bible College) and his Dutch wife, Riet, became the next Principal, followed by Alex Awad, Bishara's brother and his wife Brenda, and finally the last Principal I shared the work with was Brice Brenneman and his Palestinian wife Lydia Kuttab with their children Jonathon and Jameel. Brice and Lydia became the joint Principals until 1992 when all four of us moved on to other callings.

Reflecting on my time at Hope School it has become clear that not only has God raised up local Palestinians to undertake the tasks of educating and caring for the young people who live in the Bethlehem area but that he has brought Christians from all over the world to stand beside and support them as they live their lives caring for others in what is far from an easy environment. I am pleased to say that Hope School continues under the leadership of:
Khader Saba – Chair Person
Dr Jihan – Headmistress
Leila Nour – Fundraising and Sponsorship co-ordinator. Leila's father, Suliman Nour, became Principal after I left.

There is one additional ministry to the school for it now also has a Kindergarten section. To quote the Chair Person, Khader Saba –

'Despite all of the personal misfortunes, sufferings and daily difficulties, the measureless source of our joy is in the fount of eternal HOPE! Yes indeed, HOPE is given to those young children in our care.'

Finally, I quote the words of a song which was popular in my youth –
'Jesus loves the little children
All the children of the world
Red and yellow, black and white
All are precious in His sight
Jesus loves the children of the world'
Yes, even the Palestinian children who live in and around the town of Bethlehem where He played as a little child before His family had to flee as refugees to Egypt.

BETHLEHEM BIBLE COLLEGE 1979 - 2019

'For God so loved the world that he gave his one and only Son, that whoever believes in him shall not perish but have eternal life. John 3v16

'Whosoever believeth in Him.' On the day of Pentecost there were Arabians present who 'did hear them speak in their own tongue the works of God,' and who heard and who believed.

Today in Bethlehem there are Arabians – Palestinian Arabs – who have heard the 'Good News' and have believed and accepted the Lord Jesus Christ as their personal Saviour.

Bishara Awad is one such believer and it was whilst he was serving the Lord as Principal of Hope Secondary School that he was given the Vision to establish a Bible College.

The College was founded in 1979 as an initiative of the local Arab Palestinian community in response to a shortage of trained workers for the local churches and Christian institutions. It has indigenous leadership and is governed by a local board of trustees representing various denominations. It is a truly interdenominational college and offers courses combining high academic standards with an encouragement to a deep spiritual commitment to Christ.

It is, however, more than just an institution, it is a centre of peace, hope and reconciliation, a place where the light of Christ shines forth into a dark and troubled world.

The courses offered at the College include: Biblical History – Content and Theology; Pastoral Ministry; Christian Education; Missions and Evangelism; Music and Counselling as well as general educational topics such as English and Biblical Languages. As well as these courses the College offers an extensive Outreach Programme:

SHEPHERD SOCIETY – Through the support of caring donors around the world, more than 13,000 local residents have benefited from humanitarian aid and job creation services since the first Intifada, 1987.

PUBLIC LIBRARY – The College makes available the resources of its library and computer lab to the public.

THE BBC CHOIR – Musically gifted students can join the acclaimed Bethlehem Bible College Choir. Known for its distinctive repertoire of Middle Eastern music, this accomplished singing group conducts concert tours worldwide, often performs locally, and has produced a number of CDs.

MASS MEDIA CENTRE – Through the Mass Media programme, area residents prepare for communications, radio and television careers and produce a weekly TV program that broadcasts hope and light to the community.

EXTENTION PROGRAMMES – Due to uncertain travel restrictions and frequently changing political conditions, the school has created extension programmes in Nazareth and Gaza for students unable to come to Bethlehem.

INTERNATIONAL STUDENT PROGRAMME – We welcome pastors, seminarians, and Bible students of all ages to come to the Holy Land and study courses on Palestinian culture, history and geography; holy land archaeology and much more. The courses are offered for groups of 12 or larger.

GUEST HOUSE – For visitors from other countries, the Bible College provides a guest house for individuals and small groups.

LANGUAGE CLASSES – The College offers courses in English, German, Arabic and Hebrew to the public.

The College has had three Campus sites since its foundation in 1979.

Site No 1

This was a classroom at Hope Secondary School, Beit Jala. This meant lectures had to be held in the evenings when the school students had finished their lessons.

Site No 2

The top floor of the Bethlehem Water Company Building on the road to Beit Sahour, just a short walk from Manger Square.

Site No 3

In September 1990 the Bible College moved to a new home on the Hebron Road. The Bible Lands Society of High Wycombe England (now known as 'Embrace') very generously allowed the Bible College free use of the three buildings which were originally the Helen Keller Home for the Blind. The buildings had been standing empty for quite a while. I was with Bishara on the afternoon of 1st September when Peter Emerson of the Bible Lands Society handed over the keys. There was a lot of work to be done but at the opening ceremony in the spring of 1992 the transformation was incredible. The beautifully patterned tiled floors shone with new life and the big wooden doors, covered previously with paint, had been stripped to the original beauty of mahogany wood. With the additional classroom space and dormitories the College was able to increase its enrolment and expand its ministry. With the buildings, however, came a financial challenge of raising adequate funds for their outright purchase by 1995. With God's help this was finally achieved.

In 1996 Malcolm and I attended the celebration when the building was officially handed over to the Bible College. A programme was arranged and guests from all over the world arrived to join the local Palestinian Christians. Brother Andrew, from Open Doors, gave the address in English and Alex Awad in Arabic. Bishara presented token gifts to all the groups who had contributed in many ways. Helps International Ministries were thanked for the work they had done restoring the building – Malcolm's team in 1993 converted rooms into Bishara and Salwa's apartment and Eric and Gwen Kendall, along with Ken and Joyce Bird, converted rooms into shower units for the students.

After the official handover we all adjourned to the roof of the third building, where I had my apartment, and the foundation stone was laid for the new library, guest house and community room and computer centre.

In January 2000 (the Millenium) Malcolm and I, together with John and Janet Angle, stayed in the new building in the Guest House, which was appropriately named the Bethlehem Inn.

A few years later land behind the College was acquired and a new Student Centre was completed plus a new multi- purpose court. This features basketball and volleyball courts and is used by students, staff and faculty for fun, exercise and team building. Lighted for evening use, the area is beautifully landscaped with trees and bushes.

A campus to be proud of but much more than just buildings. Bishara's vision was for a strong centre for academic and spiritual excellence and reconciliation in Bethlehem; a true 'radiating star' of hope, love and peace in the Middle East.

To give him his full title Dr Bishara Awad continued to pursue his vision for Bethlehem Bible College both locally and internationally. A very strenuous programme indeed and his colleagues and friends began to suggest it was time to prepare someone to whom he could hand over the baton. Bishara wasn't in any hurry and with his lovely smile responded, 'God will supply someone when the time is right.'

Then in the Easter Newsletter of 2011 Bishara included the following paragraph –
'Many of our graduates are already actively serving the Christian community throughout the land. They are the leaders of the future. We are confident they will play a dynamic role in helping the College to emerge as a Christian institution in coming

decades. In his book 'Light Force' Brother Andrew of Open Doors recognised one of our graduates and current faculty member, Jack Sara, as a significant leader. On page 265 of the book, Jack states, "At Bethlehem Bible College we are confronted with a Biblical World View. That was when I started really studying the Bible and understanding who God is and therefore how to view life.'"

Bishara continues, 'Today Jack is a candidate for becoming the future President of Bethlehem Bible College.'

The Christmas Newsletter of 2012 is signed as follows –
God bless you all.
On behalf of Bethlehem Bible College and all our staff and faculty,
REV. JACK SARA
President

Bethlehem Bible College has ministered in the Bethlehem area for 40 years and is still continuing. With the Rev, Jack Sara at the helm and Dr Bishara Awad, President Emeritus. Bishara's viaion became reality when he was given $20 and told 'Start your Bible College, Bishara'.

During my sojourn in Bethlehem, although not actively involved, I became aware of other ministries working with children and young people.

One of these became a regular place for me to visit and encourage those who were carrying the burden of caring for and educating children and young adults who had to cope with disabilities of all kinds, and elderly blind men and ladies.

Just down the Hebron Road from the Bible College is the House of Hope for the Blind and Special Needs Children.

I would like to share their story and then conclude this section by listing several other ministries in the Bethlehem area who provide dedicated support to so many children and young people who need help.

THE HOUSE OF HOPE FOR THE BLIND
Founded by:
MISS MAY LADAH
A LADY OF VISION

Aunty May, as she was affectionately thought of by all, lost her sight when she was very young but said that 'God gave me a vision to do as much as I could for the blind.'

She was born in Joppa (Jaffa) in 1905; Palestine was then under Turkish rule.

Her parents heard of a home in Jerusalem run by a lady from England – Mary Jane Lovell, who started a home for blind girls in 1895 and in 1911 May was sent there as a resident. She learnt Braille, English and the Bible and the only wish she had then was to teach little blind ones and have a home for them. May moved to Jaffa and then Jerusalem and was asked to help an Arab lady, Miss Dafish, who had taken over the blind ministry on the death of Mary Lovell and together they moved to Bethlehem and set up home there in 1932. Slowly the home began to fill with blind children but they only took girls. In 1939 at the outbreak of the

Second World War they were asked to send the girls away but they decided, by faith, to keep the home going.

In 1948, when the British Mandate came to an end some servicemen, who were posted in Egypt and had visited the home, collected enough money to rent another building. They begged May to take in blind boys and to be their mother and in 1954 May's wish of many years ago, to teach little blind ones and have a home for them, became reality.

In a few weeks the Home had over 30 children, the oldest boy was 9, most of them came from nearby refugee homes. All the workers, housemothers and teachers in the home, were blind except for two sighted helpers.

In 1963 the Society which was supporting the work sent Aunty May to England and on her return she was shocked to find the Home had been moved to Beit Hanina, north of Jerusalem, and to be told that society would now be taking on the work as they felt that the authorities and the relatives of the boys would not agree to teaching the children the Bible, as she was doing.

That did not deter her; she returned to Bethlehem, rented a small two-roomed house and took in ten little orphan sighted girls. However, as new blind boys started coming to the Home she had to make new arrangements for the girls. With the coming of the boys her ministry really took off with the help of Christine David, a widow who became the Housekeeper of the House of Hope for the Blind and remained in that role for over 50 years. Christine's son Michael became involved and eventually became the Director of the Home, until his untimely death.

In 1975 Aunty May stepped out in faith and obtained a property on the Hebron Road and slowly but surely funds came in for new buildings to be built on the site.

Aunty May became the Mother of the Home, her main task was to pray for all involved in the ministry and her door was always open to cheer up big and small and help them with their problems. She continued her role until 1993 when during Evening Devotions on Thursday 4th November she had her vision fulfilled – 'To see Christ her Saviour, face to face.'

Her funeral service held on 6th November 1993 at Baraka Bible Presbyterian Church, Bethlehem, was attended by her House of Hope family and friends. In brilliant sunshine her body was laid to rest to the singing of her favourite hymns, one in particular being 'What a friend we have in Jesus.'

I was not able to attend her funeral as I was taking a sabbatical year in England but I thank the Lord that I was able to attend her Memorial Service on Sunday 27th February 1994 (her birthday) and be part of a large congregation of people who represented organisations throughout the world who had gathered to celebrate the work of May Ladah, a true saint of God.

THREE SUPPORTIVE MINISTRIES

As I have already stated, throughout time God has drawn people from around the world to support, encourage and stand beside the people of Bethlehem. He is still doing so today and I would now like to introduce three ministries who came into being during my time there and who still are very much involved in caring for those Palestinians who desperately need help in their very difficult circumstances. They are:

1. HOPE CHRISTIAN TRUST
2. MISSION TO BETHLEHEM
3. PCDC – Practical Compassion for Destitute Children

1. HOPE CHRISTIAN TRUST

I arrived at Hope School, Beit Jala, on 1st July 1982 and had plans to return to my home in Bristol early in October to fulfil a family commitment. As I settled in and got to know the needs of the School and discussed the future, Solomon Douhne suggested that it would be a good idea to get my church, St Nathanael's Anglican Church in Redland, involved in the School. They were already sponsoring me. We decided that during my stay Solomon would come to meet with the vicar, Ray Brazier, and Elizabeth his wife and congregation. The outcome of the visit resulted in the formation of Friends of Hope School who would promote the school and channel the contributions for those who wished to sponsor a student or give financial help.

On my return to the School I received a letter from John and Janet Angle who had heard about the School and Bible College and me from a friend who had visited both establishments with a group from Trinity College, Bristol.

The letter said that they would be in Jerusalem for the New Year of 1983 with two friends and would it be possible for them to visit us in Bethlehem. Naturally we said yes.

So on a cold January day we collected John and Janet and Roy and Sandra Lawrence and brought them to the Bible College. As the morning proceeded the sky got darker and darker until Alex Awad, Dean of Students said, 'It is about to snow. If we don't leave now we won't be able to get up to Hope School.' Fortunately we did and then returned safely to the Bible College. From there we took them to Bishara and Salwa's home in Beit Safafa, just past the Green Line that separates Bethlehem from Jerusalem. Salwa had provided pizza and made us an English trifle for dessert. We then returned them to Jerusalem to their hotel but I had to spend the night with the Awad family as the snow made it impossible for me to get back to Beit Jala.

The four friends flew back to England, their visit having made a big impact on them, especially John and Janet. For the Lord had begun to show them that He wanted them to link up with School and College they had visited. They joined up with Friends of Hope School and eventually when the Brazier's felt they needed to hand over the administration, John and Janet took over. They changed the name to Hope Christian Trust so that the Bible College as well as other ministries in the Middle East could be included and they registered it as a charity.

The two friends who came with them on that first visit to Bethlehem, Roy and Sandra Lawrence, decided to sponsor a

student at Hope School and support the Bible College.
Hope Christian Trust's logo is RELEASING POTENTIAL.

For over 40 years now the Trust have been supporting communities and encouraging Christian ministry in Israel and Palestine.

THEY SUPPORT:
Students who are training at Bethlehem Bible College
The House of Hope for the Blind and Special Needs
The Shepherds Society who try to give aid in emergencies as well as those out of work and unable to meet medical and education expenses as well as buying food to feed their families
Isolated Christian Communities
Teacher training
Poor or displaced families
Mobility for the disabled
Christian education
Hearing impaired
Church growth

Their brochure states:
> BE A PARTNER WITH HOPE CHRISTIAN TRUST
> TOGETHER WE CAN MAKE A DIFFERENCE

Their contact address is:
The Hope Christian Trust
14 Farthing Combe
Axbridge
Somerset
BS26 2DR
E-mail: hopebethlehem@btinternet.com

2. MISSION TO BETHLEHEM

This came into being to help and support The House of Hope for the Blind and Special Needs children and adults.

In 1989, a young lady by the name of Sarah Gibby arrived at the House of Hope to work as a House Mother for the boarding children. However, I first met Sarah at the Garden Tomb in Jerusalem. I had gone to show some visiting friends around the Garden and Sarah had been taken there by some of the other House Mothers and our paths crossed. It didn't take long for our friendship to flourish and I was given the title of Auntie Lynn.

In March 1989, Sarah's parents John and Pauline (Pim to her friends) came to visit Sarah and I was introduced to them. John and Pim formed a strong bond with Auntie May, who was called Sit May in Arabic, and made many visits to the Home and actually gave up a whole year to serve at the Home. When Auntie May passed away John had the privilege of conducting her funeral service.

From those early years the seed was sown for John and Pim to lay down the foundation for Mission to Bethlehem.

Before I continue I would like to digress and introduce another fellow English man who also was led by the Lord to share in the Ministry of the House of Hope – Edgar Evans. Edgar was one of the many English servicemen who visited Auntie May at the House of Hope.

In 1951, with National Service still in force in England, he joined the RAF for three years and was posted to the Suez Canal, Egypt.

Trips were possible to Jordan because sometimes there was a spare seat on a flight to Amman and Edgar was in charge of the Group Orderly Room that organised such vacancies! Edgar's first trip fulfilled his lifelong ambition to visit the Holy Land.

He was able to take a taxi across Allenby Bridge and up the desert road to Jerusalem, staying in Christchurch Hostel in the Old City which, in 1952 together with the West Bank, was all part of Jordan. A couple of holidaying school teachers suggested to Edgar that he make his way to Bethlehem to meet a lady affectionately known as Auntie May.

Taking the bus full of shepherds and sheep to Bethlehem he found, after much searching, the Blind Home and was offered English tea with toasted teacakes! The welcome was great and it started a lifelong association with Auntie May and the House of Hope.

Edgar stated in his biography, 'I was indeed privileged to share in the work with Auntie May and her many friends and helpers. She really did teach me to pray and to expect great things from God.'

I first met Edgar and his wife Eunice at my home in Bristol when I came home for the Christmas of 1984. This came about because when Auntie May knew I was going to be in Bristol she asked me if I would take some bars of olive oil soap for Edgar and Eunice's daughter. As I usually had a list of requests from Palestinian friends and neighbours to bring back items from England I was quite happy to do things in reverse. As Edgar and his family lived in Bath it was quite easy for them to come over to collect the soap and so I, too, began a friendship with them, which involved a link with their church and my ministry at Hope School and the Bible College.

John and Pim Gibby first got to know Edgar in March 1989 when Sarah began her work as House Mother at the House of Hope, and so our ministries became intertwined.

After their year of service at the House of Hope John and Pim served a period at the Garden Tomb in Jerusalem and on their return to Wales (where they live). Mission to Bethlehem was born, spreading out into many areas, not only in Bethlehem itself but surrounding villages as well.

MISSION TO BETHLEHEM:
A MISSION OF ENCOURAGEMENT
<u>Encouragement</u> in the Village Outreach to young people with special needs and their families
<u>Encouragement</u> to the Christian Care Homes who minister to children and adults with both physical and mental special needs
<u>Encouragement</u> to Evangelical Schools who seek to educate children and young people and teach them the Word of God.
Encouragement to Churches, Bible College, Bible Bookshop and Christian Centres, that they may be faithful witnesses to the saving and keeping power of the Gospel.

'If a man's gift . . . is encouraging, let him encourage.'
(Romans Chapter 12 verses 6 & 8)

That is exactly what John and Pim Gibby have done for many years; they have seen their ministry as 'A work of faith and a labour of love.'

However, in their July 2018 Mission Report they shared that they are looking to the Lord as he unfolds His plans for the future of Mission to Bethlehem as they prepare to 'hand over the baton'; particularly in the direction of their friends, Laurence and Sharon Garnett who are leading the Love in Action charity and with whom they already have a close liaison.

Laurence and Sharon, based at Beit Yosef, have a ministry of family visitation and respite care for severely disabled young people and have already been assisting the Mission to Bethlehem with some of their work. Unfortunately, they and all their international team members have had to leave Bethlehem. This is due to the Israel Authorities not being willing to provide visas for them to continue. Laurence and Sharon are now directing the ministry and their local Bethlehem staff from the UK because it will be 12 months before they can apply to return.

The need for both of these ministries to continue is vital for they are providing support and skilled care to many severely disabled young people who, without them, would be condemned to a life without hope.

Mission to Bethlehem
12 Montana Park
Hirwaun
Aberdare
Wales CF44 9HY
E-mail: pimjohn@aol.com

PRACTICAL COMPASSION FOR DESTITUTE CHILDREN

PCDC's story began with a vision many years ago when the Reverend Malcolm S Jones was taking part in a Study Programme at St George's College in Jerusalem. As he travelled around the West Bank his heart was so moved as he witnessed the poverty and hardship that the children were suffering and in his heart he knew he had to do something to help them but how and when needed a lot of thought and prayer.

Finally the work began to unfold in December of 1995. A month after I left Bethlehem to marry my 'Malcolm Jones'. It was a few years later that we came to hear of PCDC.

Malcolm and I spent a month in Portimao, a town on the Portuguese Algarve. We attended The International Christian Fellowship and were asked if we could share about our time in Bethlehem, which we did. We returned home to Lancashire and the following year received a letter from Lois Herrington who attended the church and she told us that another gentleman, also called Malcolm Jones (co-incident or God-incident!), had also shared about his ministry in Bethlehem. Naturally we made contact and began to hear what the PCDC ministry is all about. It is hard to find words to convey the support that is given to these children; I find it most humbling and awesome.

All the helpers are volunteers from the UK, who take it in turn to go to Bethlehem for two weeks at a time, and a loyal local young man called Mahmoud.

Rather than myself trying to convey what PCDC is all about I will pass you over to the Reverend Malcolm Jones himself and let you read his 2016 Christmas Newsletter.

THE PLIGHT OF THE CHILDREN

Dear Friends

I am writing to you in a little room about 100 metres from the spot where Jesus Christ was born. PCDC is here in Bethlehem working on our third visit this year. We think of Bethlehem at Christmas: we usually sing 'O little town of Bethlehem, how still we see thee lie'. It is very different today. Bethlehem now is a vast sprawling city with houses built on every square metre of land. It is far from being a little town: and it is never still, like in the Christmas carol. Bethlehem is a noisy eastern city, with enormous traffic jams, honking cars and endless noise. Everywhere you can hear the clattering of pneumatic drills, bulldozers, cars and more cars, racing engines, and screeching tyres. There is endless noise.

Bethlehem is surrounded by a very high wall. No-one can leave the city without a permit, and these are very hard to get. Indeed, Bethlehem is often described as a large dusty prison. The dust is everywhere: it gets down our throats, parches our lips, enters our lungs. We cough all day and half the night. Into this eastern maelstrom, God chose to be born as man. The wonder of this is never absent from our hearts. Why ever did God choose to be born in this place? Here He would be surrounded by those who would oppose Him: cunning tricksters, over-holy religious people who knew better than the Son of God. Here He would be persecuted, hunted down and, as a child, would have to run for His life as a refugee. Here under the boiling sunshine, He would struggle to breathe. He was oppressed, and remained a prisoner to the strong army of those who opposed Him.

So, what's changed? Nothing much has changed. Life here is pretty much the same today. It is a real struggle. Here is a woman with three children to raise. Where is her husband? We don't know. He is simply not here. He is probably in the 'hotel' (slang for jail). She earns £400 in a small shop. She pays rent for her rodent-infested house (£200 a month), and lives on what's left. With this she must pay for electricity (much dearer than in England) and water, when it comes, is also much more expensive than in the UK. She needs food for her three little ones aged 5, 7 and 9. There is no heating in their home, high on the mountain outside Bethlehem. The children are in summer tee-shirts all the year round. Outside the temperature has dropped to 3 centigrade. It is winter. PCDC is on a routine visit. The children run to give us big hugs. We can see that they miss their Daddy. We detect that they are well below the breadline. I look around the home. There are almost no toys. In the kitchen, the fridge is empty, just a few slices of bread and some ice cubes. Clearly these children go to school hungry. They tell me that even the bus driver lets them use the bus to go to school and does not take a fare.

Time to act: we take the mother and the children to the supermarket. We help her to fill a trolley with basics and one or two luxuries. A trolley load of groceries at Aldi's back home would cost less than £50: here it comes to £146 for the same items. The 9-year old is bursting out of his trousers. They are too tight and half way up his legs. His shoes are pinching and worn. Mother has no money for new clothes. PCDC will help her to sort it out; another trip to the Bethlehem market, to Abu Rumman's. The 5-year old drives the trolley; the two trolleys. Then the trolleys drive him, down a slope. He giggles as he tries to steady them. He is a very tiny child.

I remember when he was a baby, carrying him to the doctor. He needed splints on his legs every three weeks. He had 'clicky hips'. Now he is OK, but very, very vulnerable.

We buy all the clothes that all three children will need for the winter: shirts and blouses, trousers and underclothes, pyjamas, jackets, jumpers, scarves and gloves. I stupidly have forgotten to bring my credit card. Luckily the merchant lets me pay him in Jordanian dinars as I had some with me. He is a kindly man. I pay £360 dinars. There are many charities here in Bethlehem, all doing good work. But all the charities support institutions. There is only one that people can call on when a crisis comes. PCDC will go to the house and school to sort out the problems. We will see to the rodents in the house. Paul, another trustee, is wonderful at fixing broken toilets, doors, showers. We will let the children hug us, bring them toys, play with the children, love them, listen to them, pray with them, bring Christ's love into their homes. Only PCDC does this: we work professionally, to high standards, but we do not mind getting our hands dirty and bring the love of Jesus to the broken hearts of the poor.

What a privilege!
This team is made up of Kathleen, who listens to, and prays with, the families; James, our IT man, who keeps in touch with England, and with Peter, our financial manager; Mahmoud, our faithful one-time student, now a nurse at Bethlehem Children's Hospital, who helps us with transport and translations and in many other ways so reliable; and Paul, our practical man, who likes fixing things. Then there is me: I co-ordinate the programme and work alongside all the schools and homes. Mahmoud understands the culture and

is totally trustworthy and reliable: young and strong, he is 26 years old and we are proud to have him on the team.

So here we are in Bethlehem, sending to you our love and greetings, and our prayers. Please pray also for us. Pray for the poor, the fatherless, the widows and the broken families, the sick children. When you eat your Christmas dinner, remember those who will eat rice and beans. When your children open their presents, remember those who have no toys at all. When you turn on your central heating, remember those who have no heating, or could not afford to run it.

Bless you for reading this, and for your support all the year round. God bless you for making our work here a possibility, bringing hope to the broken ones, and food to the hungry ones, clothes to the cold ones, and love to the ones whose hopes have been dashed to the ground.

We are sustaining 245 children, the latest one a child of three years, a small boy who has been abandoned. All 245 are in school with fees paid for. There is hope.

May the Christ child also bring to you hope and peace and joy this Christmastide.

With love and thanks to you all

Malcolm, PCDC

www. practical-compassion.co.uk

As I have already mentioned, Bishara Awad, President Emeritus of Bethlehem Bible College, nearly always would say to tour groups who visited the College or include in his newsletters the following statement –

'Please pray that we can keep the light of Christ shining in Bethlehem.'

On reflection and after reading through my manuscript, it seems very clear to me that the Palestinian Christians are indeed keeping that light shining. The individuals and ministries I have shared about are like candles shining in a very dark situation.

However, there are many more ministries and individuals who are also lighting candles in the Bethlehem area, plus many I don't even know about.

I conclude this section with a list of those ministries which have been brought to my attention.
If these and all the other ministries were made into one very big candle, without a doubt we can thank God that the Light of Christ is well and truly lit in the town of His birth.

THIS LITTLE LIGHT OF MINE I'M GOING TO LET IT SHINE . . .
. . . could well be the theme tune for the following institutions and organisations I haven't previously mentioned:

JEMIMA FOUNDATION
Jemima is an organization devoted to caring for people with mental disabilities on the Westbank. Local employees provide professional care, inspired by their Christian compassion. They work together with (expert) specialists from abroad, including the Netherlands.
www.jemima.eu

MA'AN lil- HAYAT

'Ma'an lil-Hayat', in Arabic: 'Together for life', is a centre in Bethlehem, where young people and adults with learning difficulties can come together, and make friends. The project is part of L'Arche Communities, an International Federation founded in France in 1964 by Jean Vanier.

They provide motivating occupational opportunities for special needs young adults, some of whom were previously in the House of Hope and House of Joy. (House of Joy was a home set up by Sarah and Sami Awad for girls with special needs who could no longer remain at the House of Hope). Sarah of course was Sarah Gibby who first came to Bethlehem to work as a House Mother at the House of Hope.

BEIT AL LIQA

Beit Al Liqa' is a Christian Community & Training Centre and is located in the centre of Beit Jala, a town just outside Bethlehem. A wide range of programmes, events and activities for young and old alike are on offer within and without its walls. Beit Al Liqa' is an oasis of peace and a place to meet the living God. www.beit-al-liqa.de

LIFEGATE REHABILITATION

The Lifegate Rehabilitation Centre opens a door to a better life for physically and mentally disabled children and youths in Beit Jala.

THE SHEEPFOLD

The Sheepfold, run by the incredible Mary Rewers, provides day care for the most vulnerable and severely disabled children and young adults. (Mary is also based in the UK at present because of visa restrictions).
www.abcdbethlehem.org/the-sheepfold

IMMANUEL CHRISTIAN BOOKSHOP

Immanuel Christian Bookshop is a place of hope and life in Bethlehem run by Rema. Based in a Moslem area, Rema gives away Bibles to those who come in enquiring about faith. The bookshop is a story of God's faithfulness amidst hardship.

BEIT IBRAHIM /ABRAHAM'S HERBEGE

Attached to the Evangelical Lutheran Church of the Reformation in Beit Jala, 40 boys live here and go to local schools and are cared for by Saba Shawan, the House Father and his team.
All these plus many Christian Schools –

Latin Patriarchate School
Jerusalem School and Miss Grace, Head Teacher
The three Lutheran Schools in the area
Ephpheta Deaf School for Children
Terra Santa School
School of Joy – Beit Sahour

PLUS

All the churches in the area –
Greek Orthodox – Lutheran – Catholic – Baraka Church – and Syrian Orthodox - Ethiopian and other.

Individual pastors like Bassam Bannora who are spreading the Gospel, day in day out.

All fulfilling the words of the children's hymn –

Jesus bids us shine, with a clear, pure light,
Like a little candle burning in the night;
In this world of darkness we must shine,
You in your small corner, and I in mine.

Author Susan Warner (1819-1885)

WHAT BETHLEHEM MEANS TO ME

Our TIME MACHINE has taken us on a visit to what was once the little town of Bethlehem and is now a large and world famous city.

We began in the MISTS OF TIME when the descendants of Caleb – Ephrathah – Hur and Salma established the little town.

We have now arrived in the 21st CENTURY A.D. and the YEAR 2019.

The following section is written by fellow compatriots of mine who I came to know, not whilst living in the UK, but in Bethlehem; each one of us having been led by the Lord to serve Him in His native town. There is one exception, Brice Brenneman and his wife Lydia. Yes, we did meet in Bethlehem but they hailed from Ohio, USA.

I now hand over to each one of them to share their thoughts on:
'WHAT BETHLEHEM MEANS TO ME'
And add a few quotes from various folk who have visited the town.

THOUGHTS ON BETHLEHEM
REV. JOHN ANGLE – CO-FOUNDER 'HOPE CHRISTIAN TRUST'

I first visited Bethlehem as a student in 1964. We travelled in an old Bristol half cab bus across Europe and Turkey through Syria and into the Hashemite Kingdom of Jordan over the River Jordan and winding our way up to the top of the Mount of Olives and seeing Jerusalem for the first time. After visiting the Old City we crossed at what was called then the Mandelbaum Gate into Israel. We travelled the land, including Gaza, following in the footsteps of Jesus. We drove into the 'little town of Bethlehem' and I remember parking the bus in Manger Square and buying falafel. The owner's son still serves the best falafel in Bethlehem to this day.

To get to Bethlehem then we had to overcome the suspicion of Muslim police who confiscated passports for sharing New Testaments in Turkey, drive through Damascus three days after a bloody coup and meander through barbed wire in Jerusalem to drive from the Old City into West Jerusalem. And of course we couldn't return the way we came; the political atmosphere of suspicion and hate necessitated us sailing out of Haifa, with our bus lifted by crane on deck, to Italy.

My second visit to Bethlehem was by land and a return sea crossing of the Mediterranean with a group of sixth formers from a Yorkshire school. A third visit was made with family several years later. But it wasn't until the fourth visit to the land that I started to really get to know Bethlehem because on that visit I fell in love not just with the place but with the people.

With my wife I met two brothers Alex and Bishara Awad. It was actually snowing in Bethlehem on a cold January day. A mutual interest in teaching the Scriptures resulted in several summers being spent in Bethlehem teaching in a new Bible College which the brothers had established. Back in England setting up a Trust to support the College resulted in many hundreds of Christians in the UK praying and supporting the College's ministry to the Palestinian Church. Support for other associated ministries like the Shepherd Society, the Hebron Evangelical School and later with Brother Andrew a Christian school and church in Gaza grew and visits to Bethlehem became more and more frequent so that some years it was at least four times!

In nearly fifty five years have I seen changes in the 'little town of Bethlehem?' In some ways, yes; in other ways, no! The 'little town' is now a big town. The tourist trade is now huge although some stay away persuaded by fear of being in the West Bank. The Christian population has drastically declined as the troubles in the region have caused them to leave for a better life, often in the USA. The refugee camps are still there and within them there is still poverty and a sense of hopelessness. With many of the young people there is a spirit of rebelliousness which results in frequent protests and Israeli retaliation with tear gas, stun guns and rubber bullets – some of this, especially Friday afternoons in the road outside the Bible College where I frequently stay.

But it is still possible to capture the peace of the Christ child in the Church of the Nativity late in the evening after the hordes of tourists have melted away to large hotels for their evening meal and in the fields on the edge of the city where shepherds 'watch their flocks'. It is still possible to feed the spirit of Bethlehem – 'The House of Bread' – with an awareness of Jesus, the Bread of Life – 'feeding on him in our hearts by faith' as I say when leading a communion service.

But peace and new life have left the birth place of the Saviour of the World, the Prince of Peace and the One who is 'the Way, the Truth and the Life'.

Evidence of the One who is the Reconciler, bringing us to God and bringing us to live in harmony with each other, is sadly little evident.

In my first visit to Bethlehem I travelled through suspicion of my faith, through the political troubles of a coup with patrols of soldiers and armed tanks, across secure borders of barbed wire only to find I had to find another way to get back home as the way I wished to go was blocked. Bethlehem today is the same. A sense of suspicion pervades. Political and family allegiances cause rifts and a lack of unity. Different religious and Christian groups strongly maintain their own identity and fail to achieve the reconciliation and unity Jesus intended. As in the book of Judges, 'everyone does that which is right in their own eyes'.

Many Christians in Bethlehem who own land in the fields and hills around had their land compulsorily taken by Israeli settlers and therefore deprived of their ancient livelihoods on the land. Justice is denied. Many Christians don't have permission to travel outside Bethlehem to visit friends and family nor to worship in Jerusalem and elsewhere. Now a wall surrounds the birthplace of Jesus. If Mary and Joseph came today there would be no access to the town, let alone a room in an inn! The wall imprisons Jesus and his 21st century followers.

But Bethlehem, as a friend said on my last visit – 'your second home' – remains the one place on earth where my heart is at rest and, yes, I feel 'at home'. Walls cannot impede the march of the life of Jesus. Injustice cannot stop the flow of hope and joy that comes from Jesus. Guns, tear gas and soldiers cannot disturb the peace that comes from the Prince of Peace born in Bethlehem. The cries and tears of those who are oppressed, disenfranchised and have land stolen from them cannot silence the song of the angels bringing 'glory to God' and 'peace and God's favour' to all. Out of 'Bethlehem in the land of Judah' Jesus has come, one 'who will be the shepherd and the ruler' of all people. The light of the world has come and all the forms of darkness that seek to overcome it will never succeed. I love Bethlehem – 'The House of Bread' – because out of this city has come The One who feeds me and our world in a totally satisfying way. Jesus is the bread of life, for all life and for every aspect of life and that happens in fellowship with wonderful friends from Bethlehem. The place, the people coming together with the Person – Jesus.

THOUGHTS ON BETHLEHEM
BY JANET ANGLE – CO-FOUNDER 'HOPE CHRISTIAN TRUST'
'O Little town of Bethlehem how still we see thee lie.'
I am thrilled to add to Lynn's book on this wonderful place that has been part of my life since my first visit in 1969. But it wasn't until 1980 that I saw that it would be part of my life's work and still is to this day.

Bethlehem, the story of Ruth and Naomi, the place of David's well and many Biblical stories. All this, yes, but to me it is 'the Womb' from where Christianity was born and to where I return time and time again. To me it is a place of beginning, a place of friendship and hospitality as I have travelled to the land over so many years. Bethlehem is always the staring point to leave from on the many visits to other towns, villages and people.

I well remember one Saturday afternoon in February when Lynn and I went to shop at five o'clock. Lynn looked at me and said, 'I know where you want to go, go on!' It was to the grotto of the Nativity. I wanted to be there on my own in the small cave lit by candles, smelling the wax, not looking at the star which is the attraction for so many pilgrims, but to sit at the back and in the dim light gaze on an old worn painting of Mary breastfeeding Jesus; a picture ignored by many. I was there in the womb all on my own. The business of people shopping was outside, but I was at peace in the silence of the moment.

'O little town of Bethlehem how still we see thee lie'.
Sadly times have changed. Tourists rush around taking photos. Many of the old shops have disappeared from the Suk, like the hardware shop where the old man asked if I could bring from England a large print Bible as his eyesight was failing. He had a Bible from the times of the Mandate. Now there are many shops selling plastic ware and plastic toys. Father Christmas has found his place in shops and streets.

With the conflict between children and soldiers by the 'Wall' a new hotel has been sprung up by Banksy. Sitting in there and looking at the artwork and the stuffed cat hanging from a bird cage I see a picture of the people of Bethlehem as it is now. Safe only if you stay within the Wall. But I like to change the picture to see a sheepfold and the shepherd of our souls keeping them safe. The picture is still on the wall of the grotto and the candle wax still fills the air so, for me, I can live in that moment and know that has not changed.

THOUGHTS OF BETHLEHEM
BY JOHN GIBBY – CO-FOUNDER 'MISSION TO BETHLEHEM'
I could not have dreamed how important Bethlehem would have become in my Christian life and ministry in the past 30 years.

Bethlehem was, of course, very prominent in my formative years as the birthplace of Jesus and I can well remember in one Sunday School Anniversary we recited:
Bethlehem the place of Blessing
And of love beyond compare,
For from Bethlehem to Calvary
Jesus went and suffered there.

So even in my youth the message of Jesus from the Cradle to the Cross and then the Crown (Philippians Chapter 2 vv 5-11) meant that Bethlehem was very meaningful to me.

I first physically visited Bethlehem on a Holy Land Tour in the wintertime of early 1988. I must say that what I actually saw in the Church of the Nativity at that time did not impress me very much. However, afterwards, when we visited the House of Hope for the Blind and Handicapped, a real sense of the true meaning of Bethlehem gripped my heart, for as we walked through the front door God spoke to me and said, 'Here in this place the Word is made flesh.'

I discovered in the House of Hope an elderly and Godly blind lady called May Lada (Auntie May) who had founded and was leading a real 'work of faith and labour of love' ministering with the compassion of Jesus to the practical and spiritual needs of many special needs people of all ages.

A year later our youngest daughter went to serve the Lord as Housemother in the House of Hope and my wife and I were soon visiting this Home in Bethlehem twice a year to support and encourage the ministry. Bethlehem therefore became increasingly important in my Christian focus and ministry, particularly because of the strong friendship I established with May Ladah and many folks who lived in the Home.

In 1994 the Lord called my wife and I to serve full time in the House of Hope, so I resigned my job, took early retirement and moved to Bethlehem. Our service in the House of Hope transformed the direction of our ministry as we became very involved with Palestinian special needs children and young people and began to visit their family homes, building relationships with them as we sought to share the love of Jesus.

After serving in the House of Hope for one year my commitment to Bethlehem was firmly established and laid the foundation for my entire subsequent ministry there which has expanded in many wonderful directions!

I gradually built up relationships with other Christian works in Bethlehem and the West Bank including Care Homes, Christian Churches, Evangelical Schools and the Bethlehem Bible College.

In 2003 my wife and I had a burden to reach out to the young people who had been in care in the House of Hope in the 1990's and were now grown adults, living back in their Muslim homes in the West Bank, many having become believers in Jesus while they were in care . . . thus Mission to Bethlehem was born!

Bethlehem now has great meaning for me because it is the place where the Lord has called me twice a year to reach out with the love of Jesus. What a privilege to be an ambassador for Christ sharing His compassion to Christian Care Homes, Evangelical Schools, families in Muslim Villages, Children and Young People with Special Needs and Individuals; 'if any man's gift . . . is encouraging, let him encourage' (Romans 12:6&8).

Serving the Lord among Palestinian people in Bethlehem and the West Bank has been, and is, an overwhelming experience. The preaching, the prayer, the laughter, the tears, the singing, the praise, the giving, the fellowship, the friends, the sympathy, the empathy, the pain, the poverty, the power, the security wall, the checkpoints, the love, the LORD, all call me too exclaim . . . Bethlehem I love you!

THOUGHTS ON BETHLEHEM
BY PIM GIBBY – CO-FOUNDER 'MISSION TO BETHLEHEM'
My first visit to Bethlehem was when my husband and I were on a Holy Land Tour to celebrate our 25th Wedding Anniversary. Since then Bethlehem has become a special place for us, not only because of the place it is but the people who live there and have become part of our lives.

Firstly, this was the place where, for me, so many of the Bible stories that took place here became a reality. Naomi and her daughter-in-law, Ruth, who married Boaz from Beit Sahour (Shepherd's Field); David, the great grandson of Ruth and Boaz, because he trusted God took on Goliath the Giant and was victorious. Later, when he was hiding from King Saul, who wanted to kill him, found his faithful band of men had crept back into Bethlehem to get him his heart's desire, water from the well at Bethlehem.

It was here in Bethlehem that Bible prophesies were fulfilled when the Angels appeared to the Shepherds in those Bethlehem fields and told them of the birth of the Saviour, Jesus Christ the Lord. The wonder of that birth, God becoming man, born to die the death on Calvary to take away my sin so that I could be set free and have a personal relationship with the Lord Jesus, here was where that human story had its beginning.

Secondly, Bethlehem was the place where I met a wonderful lady called Aunty May Ladah. Blind from the age of five she had a God-given vision to make a home for blind children. This she accomplished and eventually the home was known as the House of Hope. This dear lady taught me so much over the years about Faith. What an example of simple trust in a Heavenly Father who she could talk to at any time about anything knowing He heard and would answer. As she could tell Him all her problems and needs there was no need to tell anyone else and He never, never failed her.

Thirdly, Bethlehem is the place where, over the years, we have met so many wonderful children, all with learning disabilities, yet they have a great capacity to respond to the love of Jesus and to show that love to others. These children, now in their twenties and thirties, have become part of our life. We continue to visit Bethlehem regularly and keep in contact with these young people and help to support their families in practical ways. They are now living back in their Muslim villages but they are maintaining their simple love for Jesus and that brings great joy to our hearts. Thank you, Lord Jesus, for Bethlehem and all the Lambs that you are still shepherding in the land of your birth.

MEMORIES OF BETHLEHEM
BY BRICE BRENNEMAN – CO-DIRECTOR 'HOPE SCHOOL'
In the summer of 1990 my wife Lydia, a Palestinian Christian born in Bethlehem, and I, along with sons Jonathan aged 2 and Jameel aged three months, began a two-year assignment as co-directors of Hope Secondary School just outside Bethlehem. For my wife this was a bit of a homecoming, but for me this represented a very dramatic change having spent almost my entire life in the state of Ohio.

One of the things that struck me right away was how casually the local Palestinian population used the term Bethlehem. To them it was a local town/city where you went to conduct business, buy groceries, see a doctor, or have employment. In a month or two I also found myself viewing Bethlehem as just another West Bank city.

Over the last three years Lydia and I have led two tour groups on trips that try to provide a roughly equal portion of viewing of Holy Land sites and seeing firsthand what the plight of the Palestinians living under Israeli occupation really is. Staying in Bethlehem and seeing the major holy sites in the area has had a special meaning to those on our trips. While I enjoy seeing our friends' reactions to the sights I have personal memories of our time in Bethlehem that are more significant to me.

During the two years Lydia and I spent at Hope School we worked side by side with two remarkable people who had been at Hope School for eight years. George Shawrieh, a Christian Palestinian and Hope School alumni had the title of school secretary. Secretary there meant running all aspects of the business side of the school, keeping records, filing reports, assisting with discipline, and giving excellent advice to me when I would ask him on an almost daily basis, 'George, what do we do about this?' He did this with a spirit of service and dedication.

While George occupied a small office on one side of me, Lynn Weaver who hailed from Bristol, England and had the title of volunteer correspondence secretary, occupied the office on the other side. Eight years earlier, she had felt a specific call to come and work somewhere in Bethlehem. It is hard to imagine someone more dedicated, capable, or easier to work with than Lynn.

Our two years at Hope School were extremely busy and they did fly by. At one point Lynn started using the word 'team' to describe how the four of us worked together. It was a team in the very best sense of the word. In my final newsletter from the school, I remember writing that I would probably never again have a work situation where I would be involved with such capable and compatible people.

I am so thankful for the experience of working closely with Lydia, George and Lynn for two years and seeing daily demonstrations of what it means to follow the Christ born in Bethlehem. That is my most significant memory of Bethlehem.

POSTSCRIPT (BY LYNN WEAVER JONES)
I feel I have no choice, even without permission, to add my own comments to Brice's contribution. Yes, we were indeed a TEAM, purely the result of Brice and Lydia's attitude and dedication towards all those who were part of Hope School –

The Teaching Staff
The Domestic Staff
and last but no means least
The Students

They treated everyone equally and in return were loved by all. This love was a visible expression of how God loves each one of us.

Their example will remain with me always.
Lynn

SNIPPETS OF BETHLEHEM REMEMBERED - HELEN FREY

"Glad you are writing about Bethlehem. It is a City that impressed me very much. Since visiting it I have never been the same!"

Helen Frey, the wife of Marvin Frey, who together stayed at Hope School as guests. Marvin wrote many hymns, now sung around the world, especially the little chorus – 'He is Lord'. They were both very much moved when they heard it sung in Arabic, at the Church of God youth meeting in Beit Jala.

"I was so blessed to be able to spend 9 months in 1980/81 and another 2½
years from January 1983 – June 1985 at the HOLY FAMILY CHILDREN'S HOME in Bethlehem as a volunteer. (The babies that were brought to the Home had, most often, been abandoned or the mother was unable to care for them.)
I helped care for the 2-5 year olds and then the babies. I worked with other volunteers from various countries which was an incredible experience. Not knowing Arabic or French, the common languages of the Sisters who ran the home, was a great lesson in the universal language of love. A simple smile or hug or greeting in another language meant a lot to them and made me 'forget' that I couldn't communicate much verbally but that I could in other ways. The children were so open and loving – what a joy – for the most part!
I had many lessons to –'TRUST GOD ALONE' and was just blessed in many ways beyond words to express."
Shirley Welch

<u>Our visit to Bethlehem December 2017</u> *by Geof and Ruth Woodhall*

Note from Editor

(My husband knew Ruth as a little girl, growing up on a farm in the Ribble Valley in Lancashire. Her father had a little 'Chapel' in the corner of one of his fields and Malcolm would occasionally speak there. Consequently, when I came to the Ribble Valley I got to know Ruth and her husband Geof. When I knew they were visiting Bethlehem in 2017 I asked for an update on the situation and knew it had to be included in this book).

"We have just returned from a holiday to Palestine and Israel. We stayed at St. Vincent's Guest House, not far from Hope School and Bethlehem Bible College and behind 'the wall'. We heard from families as to how they lived there.

Mostly without running water, apart from sometimes during the night, when they have to get up and wash their clothes. There is poverty, lack of infrastructure, rubbish everywhere and not much work. They cannot visit Jerusalem apart from twice a year at Christmas and Easter, by obtaining a special visa.

It is a very sad situation for the Palestinians. We certainly didn't see the' little donkey on the dusty road' but we did walk the oldest streets in Bethlehem on which Mary and Joseph must have walked to the Inn. Nor could we imagine the 'O Little Town of Bethlehem'. Today it is hugely built up and so busy with tourists in Manger Square. It certainly wasn't a bit as we imagined, especially being surrounded by the dreadful wall. It must be so difficult to bring up a family there. They live under siege, don't they? Such a struggle for the Palestinians.

We really enjoyed going to the Shepherd's Fields. The church on the hill was so peaceful and we all started singing 'While

Shepherds Watched' and it was so moving. We also enjoyed going into the caves where we could 'smell sheep'. No green grass, though.

[Editor's note: obviously the first rains of the year had not arrived in December. To see the green fields and cultivated fields in the spring is something to behold.]

Finally, we were amazed to see how many groups from different countries were there, singing praises to God in their native tongues. We felt it was a foretaste of Heaven.

To sum up our visit to Bethlehem – it was such a precious joy to have experienced the atmosphere and we have brought back lots of memories and feel that the Bible has been brought to life for us."

<u>Volunteers in Mission</u> – *Frederick and Laura Ann Zahn,* Missouri, USA

Frederick and Laura Ann spent a year as volunteers at Bethlehem Bible College 1994/5 and were a great support to me practically as well as personally.

One of the tasks we did together was to go to Issa's Olive Wood Co-operative and obtain supplies of olive wood for sale in the Bible College Souvenir Shop.

Issa's Co-operative is in Beit Sahour and several olive wood carvers sell their products through the Co-operative. Issa's own father, before his death, carved the most beautiful and intricate Christmas tree ornaments in olive wood. He was the inspiration for the Co-operative to come into being.

On their return to the USA the Zahn's, together with their son Andrew, set up a ministry importing olive wood items from Issa's Co-op and selling them, mostly at Methodist Churches and conferences. Since they began in 1996 they have raised many dollars. The profits from the sales have been sent to ministries in Bethlehem and other parts of the West Bank; most certainly an expression of love to the Palestinian people.

As well as the Olive Wood Ministry, Frederick and Laura Ann have organised Volunteers in Mission trips to Bethlehem Bible College, to give volunteers hands-on experience of mission. The volunteers get involved with the day to day ministry of the College, including practical work on the Campus.

The following is an extract of the newsletter from the twelfth VIM team to visit Bethlehem in which 14 people took part:

"As well as working at the College we visited Issa and his family and enjoyed a meal with them.
We also visited the Tent of Nations at Tony and David Nasser's Farm just south of Bethlehem.

We were then blessed to have Bishara Awad, the tour host at the College. Of course, he did an awesome telling of the story of the College and his own family testimony.
Our final stop was with Bishara's son, Sami Awad, at the Holy Land Trust Office (a peace initiative). The entire team truly appreciated his explanation of the ministry and his telling of the history of the conflict and its root problems.

We were able to deliver donations as usual from our olive wood ministry, to the value of $26,000.

From my own experience of looking after volunteer groups who came to the College I know that without a doubt that both the team members and the Palestinian Christians they were involved with were all richly blessed."

Frederick and Laura Ann first visited Bethlehem as volunteers on a VIM team led by Bob Younts but for them it was not to be a once in a lifetime experience. For over 35 years they have allowed God to use them to serve Palestinians not only in Bethlehem but also in the village of Aboud near Tel Aviv. They have done what Brother Andrew stated in his foreword to my book, 'Who From Our Mother's Arms', and that is –

'They have got personally involved, without choosing sides. They have gone and found people in Bethlehem, got close to them, they have listened and yes, above all else, they have offered them their hearts, their hands and their shoulders for them to cry on.'

As this section closes I can also say that the above quotation applies also to John and Janet Angle of Hope Christian Trust; John and Pim Gibby of Mission to Bethlehem; Rev Malcolm Jones and his team Practical Compassion for the Destitute Children; plus all those who at this time are serving those in need in Bethlehem.

THE STAR STILL SHINES

Countless Christmas songs and Christmas carols have been written over the centuries and in many, many languages. Christians around the world love to sing them and everyone has their own special favourite. Without a shadow of doubt, my favourite carol has to be 'O Little Town of Bethlehem' followed closely by 'O Holy Night, the stars are brightly shining, it is the night of the dear Saviour's birth.'

As Christmas Eve approaches we sing them in our homes, we hear them as we do our shopping in the stores and markets, we go to carol concerts in churches, in schools and in our places of work. We sing them by candlelight and join in with the carol singers who knock on our door. Some of us sing them when we go to see our children perform in the nativity play reminding us of that very first Christmas night when our Lord Jesus Christ was born, in a stable, in Bethlehem.

Christmas carols and the town of Bethlehem are synonymous. It would be simply impossible to reproduce them in this little book. However, I would like to include three Christmas poems which have been written about Bethlehem and Christmas, two of which are themed on the Christmas story and one which applies to Christmas in Bethlehem in 2018.

I also include the story of St. Jerome's Cave which is a cave in the same complex as the cave which would have been the stable in which Jesus was born.

HOW FAR IS IT TO BETHLEHEM?

Words by Frances Chesterton (1869-1938)

How far is it to Bethlehem? Not very far. Shall we find the stable-room Lit by a star?

Can we see the little Child? Is He within? If we lift the wooden latch, May we go in?

May we stroke the creatures there — Ox, ass, or sheep? May we peep like them and see Jesus asleep?

If we touch His tiny hand, Will He awake? Will He know we've come so far Just for His sake?

Great kings have precious gifts, And we have naught; Little smiles and little tears Are all we brought.

For all weary children Mary must weep; Here, on His bed of straw, Sleep, children, sleep.

God, in His mother's arms, Babes in the byre, Sleep, as they sleep who find Their heart's desire.

THE LITTLE ROAD TO BETHLEHEM
Words by Margaret Rose (d 1958)

As I walked down the road at set of sun
The lambs were coming homewards one by one
I heard a sheepbell softly calling them
Along the little road to Bethlehem
Beside an open door as I drew nigh
I heard sweet Mary sing a lullaby
She sang about the lambs at close of day
And rocked her tiny King among the hay

Across the air the silver sheepbells rang
"The lambs are coming home," sweet Mary sang
"Your star of gold, your star of gold is shining in the sky
So sleep, my little King, go lullaby"
As I walked down the road at set of sun
The lambs were coming homewards
one by one I heard a sheepbell softly calling them
Along the little road to Bethlehem.

CHRIST AT THE CHECKPOINT

a poem written by Elias, a young Palestinian Christian from Bethlehem. He hosts the weekly 'Make a Difference' radio show, profiling the community work of local Christian ministries. He also records many of the devotions that speak a Christian perspective into everyday life in Bethlehem.

If I am a Christian it means that Jesus is with me.
Wherever I go I take Jesus with me.
When I am on the bus, Jesus is right with me.
When I am walking on the street with my friends, there is Jesus.
When I go to the checkpoint and get frustrated because of all the time wasted, Jesus is with me.
When I have to take off my shoes and belt and go under the scanner, Jesus is right there with me.
Everywhere we go we represent Jesus in our life.
If someone wants to know Jesus, they should be able to look at my life and see Jesus in me.
When the soldier stops you on the street, what does he see?
Does he see anger, bitterness and resentment?

Does hatred shine through towards him?
Or does he see the love of Jesus in your eyes?
It's Jesus in you that will speak into his heart and life.
Let Jesus live through you!

The inhabitants of Bethlehem, Muslim and Christian alike, undergo frequent humiliations and discomforts as a result of the Israeli Military occupation. Despite the many hardships – to which the natural human response is anger, frustration, and even hatred – Elias' poem beautifully and succinctly encapsulated the Messiah's response we are called to espouse as believers.

St Jerome's Cave

From a cave beneath the Church of the Nativity in Bethlehem came the most enduring version of the Bible ever translated.
In this underground study — pleasantly cool in summer but chilly in winter — St Jerome spent 30 years translating the Scriptures from Hebrew and Greek into Latin, the language of the common people.

The scholarly Dalmatian priest began his task around AD 386. The text he produced in St Jerome's Cave was the first official vernacular version of the Bible. Known as the Vulgate, it remained the authoritative version for Catholics until the 20th century.
This version, asserts the historian G. S. P. Freeman-Grenville, was "assuredly heard by more Christians than any other".
St Jerome (also known as Hieronymus, the Latin version of Jerome) spent more than 36 years in the Holy Land. He was well-known for his ascetic lifestyle and his passionate involvement in doctrinal controversies.

Access to St Jerome's two-room cave is from the Church of St Catherine. On the right hand side of the nave, steps lead down to a complex of subterranean chambers. At the end, on the right, are the rooms where Jerome lived and worked.

The adjacent caves have been identified as the burial places of Jerome (whose remains were later taken to Rome), his successor St Eusebius, and Sts Paula and Eustochium.

Paula, a noble Roman widow, and her daughter, Eustochium, worked with Jerome in making Bethlehem a great monastic centre.

The first cave on the left at the bottom of the stairs is identified as the Chapel of the Holy Innocents. This is said to be the burial place of infants killed by King Herod in his attempt to eliminate the newborn "King of the Jews".

Jerome wrote of innumerable pilgrims flocking to Bethlehem from Britain and India, Pontus (a part of Asia Minor, now in Turkey) and Ethiopia.
His opinion of them fluctuated, as shown by two conflicting statements:

- "The very best of the Christian community comes to the Holy Land; they speak different tongues, but the devotion is one and the same. There is no sign of conflict or arrogance, no differentiation whatsoever, except in the mode of dress. No one censures another, no one criticises or judges his neighbour."
- "They come here from all over the world, the city regurgitates every type of human being; and there is an awful crush of persons of both sexes who in other places you should avoid at least in part but here you have to stomach them to the full."

Jerome died in 420. His body was later transferred to Constantinople and then to Rome, where his bones rest today in the Basilica of St Mary Major.

In front of the Church of St Catherine, his statue stands on a granite column in a restored Crusader cloister. At his feet is a skull, a symbol of the transience of human existence.

From: http://www.seetheholyland.net/st-jeromes-cave/

In my foreword at the beginning of this anthology I shared why Epiphany meant so much to me. Not only because it is the celebration of the visit of the Magi to see and worship the baby King Jesus, but because of one of the hymns we sing at this time, 'Earth has many a noble city, Bethlehem thou dost all excel'; the hymn which God used to show me that He wanted me to leave my father's house, my family and my friends and GO to that city. The why and wherefore that all that meant for me I have endeavoured to share in this book.

I know that I am not alone, I'm sure, in thinking that Epiphany has a very important place in the calendar of the Church and as I started the book talking about Epiphany so I would like to bring it to its conclusion with thoughts on the same subject.
However, they are not my thoughts but those of Rev. Enid Briggs, known affectionately to many as Mother Enid. The first sermon I ever heard her preach was at an Epiphany Service at St Mary's Church, Mellor and I knew without a shadow of a doubt that her sermon was the perfect ending to the anthology on Bethlehem that God had shown me he wanted me to write. Mother Enid graciously gave me permission to do so.

I must say at this point it has been a daunting task for me to compile this anthology, with many obstacles in my way. Only with God's gently prodding and provision in providing help when I needed it and bringing ideas and thoughts to my mind to encourage me to keep going have I been able to finish it.

Now I place it into His hands to use it as He desires, for it is His book.

MOTHER ENID'S THOUGHTS ON EPIPHANY

"I love Epiphany! I loved Epiphany before I knew it was Epiphany. I love Christmas cards with the Three Wise Men on. I love the gold – the gold star, the kings' crowns, the golden gifts. The rich colour – the kings' robes, the camels' trappings. The hot desert, contrasted with 'the bleak midwinter'. Mysterious, exotic visitors, arriving in the night.

A wonderful story!

Actually, it isn't. It's a strange, frightening story. It has terrible consequences: as a direct result of the visit of the Magi, Mary, Joseph and Jesus have to flee the country, leaving many of baby Jesus' contemporaries in Bethlehem to be brutally murdered in his place.

Perhaps the Wise Men weren't so wise after all. Perhaps they should have stayed at home – sent a 'New Baby' card and left it at that.

This story may be nicely wrapped in gold paper – but we need to open it up and see what's inside. First, let's throw out some misconceptions.

Who were these Visitors? Matthew is our only source for this story. His account is all we have: if you haven't just heard it, it's been added much later; so, no kings, certainly no fancy names – Gaspar, Melchior and Balthasar – and no camels.

Three? Matthew doesn't say how many. Eastern Orthodox tradition says 12. The 'three' comes from the three types of gifts which Matthew mentions – gold, incense and myrrh.
Wise? Yes. Matthew's Greek word can be translated as Wise People, Sages or Magi – a word we use only in this context today. Custodians of secret knowledge. Our word magician comes from the same root as Magi.

Magi were originally a tribe of hereditary priests from the ancient Persian Empire. They were the academics, the intellectuals, the archivists; learned advisors to the Persian Emperors, doctors, philosophers, seekers after truth. They studied the stars, so they were scientists, astronomers. As the belief was – that the heavens influenced events on earth, yes – they were astrologers – but they didn't do daily horoscopes in the tabloids! And scientific study led them not to atheism, but to worship. Wise? Yes.

Where did they come from? Crib sets these days often have an Oriental, complete with turban, a Caucasian, and a Negro. Very politically correct. But Matthew says 'they returned to their country' – one country, so probably one nationality. And the African has to go – Matthew says 'they came from the east', and Africa is southwest of Israel.

Yes, they probably came from the Persian Empire, which stretched from the eastern borders of the Holy Land, through modern Iraq and Iran, and was finally halted, like so much, in the treacherous mountains of Afghanistan. The Roman and the Persian Empires met at the borders of Israel. For the time being, the Romans chose to go no further east, and the balance between the two Empires was held. But news of a powerful Jewish king who might tip that balance would be good news to the Persians. He would be a good horse to back, politically. No harm in getting in first with the presents.

When did they arrive? Herod had children up to the age of two killed. This might suggest a two-year journey but more likely Herod was erring on the safe side. It would take a few weeks along the trade routes from Persia. The Holy Family was still in Bethlehem. But the Magi arrived in Jerusalem after Jesus' birth – so they didn't arrive in Bethlehem with the shepherds. And they came to a house – no stable or manger.

Another huge misconception is that they followed 'yonder star over field and fountain, moor and mountain' –no. They 'saw his star in the east'. To astronomers this means that they saw it rising, then lost it as it 'set' over the western horizon. There are many theories about what they saw, but whatever they saw, it was something very unusual, very special – the event of a lifetime.

They set off west, not so much looking for, and certainly not following, the star but, working on their knowledge of ancient prophecies, making for Jerusalem – because that is where they would expect to find a Jewish prince. They saw a sign, looked up the information and set off for Jerusalem expecting to join the throngs of people celebrating around the royal palace. They got there – AND NO-ONE KNEW A THING ABOUT IT! Had they got it wrong??

They caused enough of a stir for Herod to hear about it. He was disturbed. There was only room for one King of the Jews in his books. And if he was disturbed, every reason for Jerusalem to be disturbed. The massacre at Bethlehem probably involved around 20 infants. Had Herod ordered a similar cull in Jerusalem, who knows how many that would have been.

The Jews themselves would never have used the term King of the Jews. That's the phrase of the Magi – and the phrase of Pontius Pilate. They used the word Messiah. And those who knew their scriptures knew that the Messiah would be born in Bethlehem. Herod sent the Magi off secretly: he didn't want half of Jerusalem following them the five miles to Bethlehem. He reckoned he could keep tabs on them from that distance, and he ordered them to report back to him.

The Magi had seen this tremendous sign. They'd come to the royal city to be a part of something earth-shattering. Now they were being sent to poke around in a tiny village. Well, having come so far, it was worth a try. They set off, AND THE STAR RE-APPEARED!

It seemed to lead them the last few miles, and it hovered directly above the house where Jesus was. Matthew says, 'When they saw the star, they were overwhelmed with joy.' And well they might be! They knelt down and paid him homage. They opened their treasure-chests and it's lavish! – gifts of gold, and incense, and myrrh. Somehow, it seems to suggest more than one of each, it suggests abundance. But why has Matthew picked out these particular items – so very unsuitable for babies?

GOLD – is for a King. International currency. The purest standard, impossible to degrade. Jesus is a King.

INCENSE – is offered by a Priest, to a God. The scented smoke billows up, representing prayers – rising to God. Jesus is both High Priest and God.

MYRRH – is for one who will die. It's thick, sticky resin which was mixed with oils and used in medicine and embalming. 33 years later, Joseph of Arimathea and Nicodemus brought myrrh and aloes to embalm Jesus. Jesus was born to die.

This is a very odd combination of gifts for the magi to come up with. Maybe Matthew used hindsight in drawing attention to these particular gifts. Or maybe the Magi simply brought the tools of their trade, their monetary, their priestly and their medicinal treasures – the most precious things they had.

The Season of Epiphany is the second, and longer, part of the 40 days from Christmas to Candlemas, the 2nd February: 12 Days of Christmas and 28 days of Epiphany.

Epiphany means 'Manifestation, making known, proclaiming, revealing'. More precisely, the Epiphany is the Manifestation of Jesus to the Gentiles. He was revealed, first, to Jewish shepherds. The Magi were the first non-Jews to worship him.

But why is Matthew interested in Gentiles? He's the one who writes as a Jew, for Jews. Matthew is stressing that salvation comes through the Jews. The Magi had to come to Israel.

So, what is it all about, this story? To Matthew, it's the glory of God breaking out in the birth of his Son. Creation overflows with joy, like the angels on the hillside. One particular star shines so brightly that it's noticed. And sincere 'seekers after truth' take up the trail and are rewarded with a glimpse of God. But it's 30 years too soon, and the 'leak' results in exile and atrocity. Matthew doesn't ask whether it was worth it or not.

What's it all about – for us? Now we've pulled the story to bits, thrown out the things that don't belong, leaving a story with a grim sting in its tail – do I still love Epiphany? Oh, yes. Because I am a Gentile. Here, my God was revealed to ME. Yes, stars should have moved. I hope that I would have read the sign, made the journey, given the most precious things I had.

I – we – still have that opportunity. Our lives are like the Magi's journey. God spoke to astrologers by a star – he met them where they were. And he meets us where we are – meets us in our ordinary, messed-up, chaotic lives. He meets us, prompts us, and sets us on a journey. Calls us to lay at his feet our most precious gifts, all that we have and are, all our plans, all our hopes, our futures, our lives.

But most of all I love Epiphany because this story is about faith, and hope, and promise. It's about a star that disappears. The Magi didn't hear Jesus speak, didn't see him raise Lazarus, didn't witness the Resurrection. But they had faith in the Light, even when it went out; in the Glory of the Lord, when they couldn't see it.

We, like them, have to carry on in faith

- when the star disappears
- when we seem to have got it wrong
- when we seem to be in the wrong place
- when no-one understands

And, if we keep faith, at the end of our journey, we will see the Glory, and we will see Jesus. Amen." Mother Enid.

EPILOGUE

I began this book with the Biblical History of the Little Town of Bethlehem. As the book progressed I began to understand the importance of the town in God's plan for mankind and for Jesus Himself.

BETHLEHEM points us to JERUSALEM

JERUSALEM points us to CALVARY

CALVARY points us to THE GARDEN TOMB

THE GARDEN TOMB points us to THE RESURRECTION

THE RESURRECTION points us to THE MOUNT OF OLIVES

THE MOUNT OF OLIVES points us to THE ASCENSION

when Jesus ascended back to heaven.

Finally, THE ASCENSION points us back to EARTH and that moment in time which tells us of Jesus' return to EARTH.
Acts Chapter 1 verses 10 & 11

And while they were gazing intently into heaven as He went, behold two men in white robes suddenly stood beside them who said, 'Men of Galilee, why do you stand gazing into heaven? This same Jesus, who was caught away and lifted up from among you into heaven, will return in the same way in which you saw Him go into heaven.'

None of these events could have taken place without the birth of that little baby, Jesus, born in a stable because there was no room for His earthly family, in the inn – in the LITTLE TOWN OF BETHLEHEM.

A TOUR OF BETHLEHEM'S BIBLICAL SITES

Rachel's Tomb

As it stands today however it is not visible from the road as the Separation Wall has been built around it.

DAVID'S WELL in the Old City where his men risked their lives to get David the drink of water he craved when he was a fugitive in the desert. When David was told what they had done he felt the water was so precious he couldn't drink it and he poured it out as a drink offering to God.

THE CHURCH OF THE NATIVITY - MANGER SQUARE

Built on the site of the first Church built by St-Helena marking the place of the birth of Jesus underneath the Church is a labyrinth of caves. 'The Stable' as we know it, was in fact, a cave where animals were kept.

Top row -
The Star that marks the place where Jesus was born.
A view of the Judean hills from the roof.
Bottom row -
The interior of the Church.
The exterior showing the bell tower

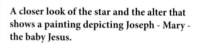

A closer look of the star and the alter that shows a painting depicting Joseph - Mary - the baby Jesus.

An historic renovation of the Church of the Nativity began in 2013, a year after Unesco declared the Church a World Heritage Site, revealing ancient mosaics and columns restored to their origianl state for the first time in 600 years.

The Palestinian Authroity appointed a committee of local Christians to oversea the work. The chairperson of the committee, Ziad al-Bandak, reported that since the work started 5 years ago, £14 million has been raised out of the £17 million needed to complete the restoration. The funding has come from the Palestinian Authority, (over half) and the rest from local Muslim and Christian businesses and the rest from foreign donors.

A WIDER TOUR OF WHAT IS A TRULY
THE CITY OF BETHLEHEM

On leaving Manger Square one exit leads up stone steps to the Souk or Market

Lynn buying her Pitta Bread back in the 1980's

Futher up the stone steps vendors sell fruit, vegetables, meat, coffee, tea, pots and pans, clothes, shoes and so much more.

Bethlehem Skyline
'But you, Bethlehem Ephrathah, though you are small among the clans of Judah, out of you will come for me one who will be ruler over Israel...'. (Micah 5:2) Please pray for the community of Bethlehem and for those who live in difficult cirumstances.

Our tour of Bethlehem comes to an end with a fairly recent building in Manger Square - the Peace Centre. Built just a few yards from the place where Jesus - The Prince of Peace was born. All the inhabitants of Bethlehem today long for their city to be at peace.

Bethlehem Peace Center
Blessed are the peacemakers, for they will be called sons of God. (Matthew 5:8)
Bethlehem Peace Centre is a cultural center with the aim to promote peace, democracy,
religious tolerance and cultural diversity. It is located in the city of Bethlehem next to Mager
Square between the Church of the Nativity and the Mosque of Omar.

THE WALL SURROUNDING BETHLEHEM

These photographs just show a little of what life is like in Bethlehem today. The wall cuts off families from each other - from their Olive groves - from their sheep and goats and from visiting Jerusalem - to gain access they need permission and then to go through a checkpoint manned by soldiers.

Graffiti on the Wall

THE SHEPHERD'S FIELD

Another exit from Manger Square leads you down and down until you reach the village of Beit Sahour (House of the Shepherd). Past the houses into an area of arable and grassland where modern day shepherds look after their flocks and farmers till the soil in mush the same way they have done for years.

It was here that Ruth gleaned the corn in the field of Boam and where the shepherds tended their sheep on the night the angels appeared to them.

Preparing the land ready to sow the crops

Looking up to Bethlehem - the City on the hill

PAINTINGS IN THE CHAPEL
AT THE SHEPHERDS FIELDS

The Angel brings glad tidings of great joy.

There they found Joseph and Mary and the Babe in a stable.

Then they returned praising the Lord and telling everyone what they had seen.

BETHLEHEM CRAFTS
'Needlework - Traditional and Modern'

Taken at the entrance to Jasser's Palace, an important and architectural building. The Palestinian women are wearing traditional clothes.
The card was prepared and produced by Maha Saco, Bethlehem and the photograph taken by Nabil Diek

Very old traditional

Modern - Biet Jala Work,
Lynn in her wedding dress

Traditional Needlework,
modern design

OLIVE WOOD CARVING

Bethlehem Artisans keep the Olive wood carving alive through life-like carvings of Jesus - The Nativity and Biblical heroes as well as carving camels, donkeys and Christmas tree ornaments

Issa Musleh at work in his new workshop

BETHLEHEM BIBLE COLLEGE

The building started out as a private residence, then became the
Helen Keller Homefor the Blind and finally the Bible College

The original building

Extension

Dr. Bishara Awad, founder of Bethlehem Bible
College and his wife Salwa

Laying the foundation stone for the extension of the original buildings in the year 2000

Dr. Awad - President Emeritus viewing the progress of the new building at the rear of the exisiting college

The view across the Hebron Road from the Bible College. The wall in frontmarks excavations of the aquaduct to bring water from Solomon's pool to Jerusalem. The houses are a refugee camp

The new BBC building

The newly completed Bible College Building

MISSION TO BETHLEHEM

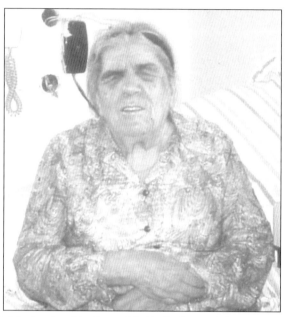

May Ladah - founder of the House of the Blind, affectionatly know as Aunty May

Lynn with Aunty May and some of the children.

Sarah Awad née Gibby - who was a housemother at the House Hope before moving with her husband Sammy Awad to run the House of Joy for special needs girls, in Beit Sahour.

Special needs children helping to get supper ready.

Yes - they do nativity plays in Bethlehem.

The older residents at work in the carpenters shop.

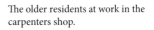

The older ladies who used to call House of Hope but who have now moved to other accommodation.

PCDC
Practical Compassion for Destitute Children at present helping 190 children in the Bethlehem area.

This is Hassan, he has 10 brothers and sisters. His Father died, he lives in destitution but loves goats and breeds them on a bit of land near the separation wall. PCDC pays his school fees and meets his medical needs.

These children need clothes for winter. So PCDS takes them shopping.

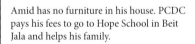

Amid has no furniture in his house. PCDC pays his fees to go to Hope School in Beit Jala and helps his family.

This is Issa, which means Jesus in Arabic. He wants to be a Greek Orthodox Priest. This is his prayer corner, his Dad helped him build it. PCDC helps ISSA to go to Hope School.

IMMANUAL CHRISTIAN BOOK SHOP
IN BETHLEHEM

Rheema who runs the book shop providing Christian books, Bibles, Children's Activity Books in Arabic and English